AGE INCLUDED

ON MUSIC, GENERATIONS, DIVERSITY, AND FREEDOM

AGE INCLUDED

ON MUSIC, GENERATIONS, DIVERSITY, AND FREEDOM

SANDRA TRIENEKENS & CONNY GROOT
EDITORS

SWP

Title	**AGE INCLUDED ON MUSIC, GENERATIONS, DIVERSITY AND FREEDOM**
Editors	*Sandra Trienekens & Conny Groot*
ISBN	978 90 8850 689 5
e-ISBN	978 90 8850 690 1
NUR	757

© 2016 SWP Publishers Amsterdam

All rights reserved. No part of this publication may be reproduced in any form without the written permission of SWP Publishers, Amsterdam, The Netherlands. Any person who does any unauthorised act in relation to this publication may be liable to prosecution and civil claims for damages.

CONTENTS

INTRODUCTION — 9
1. We Are All Included — 10
   Ger Tielen

PART I MUSIC, AGE AND DIVERSITY — 17
2. Art Projects on Age and Diversity — 19
   Sandra Trienekens & Britt Swartjes
3. Age Ain't Nothin' But a Number — 30
   Conny Groot
4. Getting to Know Music Generations — 32
   Sandra Trienekens & Milda Saltenyte
5. Art and Dementia: Inclusive and Super-Diverse — 46
   Marjolein Gysels
6. Music: Playful Power for the Personal and the Political — 52
   Eltje Bos

PART II TOWARDS POST-MULTICULUTRAL CITIZENSHIP — 67
7. 15 Years of MusicGenerations — 68
   Sandra Trienekens
8. All Included? — 104
   Zihni Özdil
9. Towards an Open Approach to Integration — 106
   Maurice Crul
10. Challenging Social Cohesion and Citizenship — 118
    Sandra Trienekens

PART III IMPLICATIONS — 143
11. Challenges for Policy, Funding, and Education — 144
    Sandra Trienekens

APPENDIXES — 151
I. Music Generations: people & figures — 152
II. About the authors — 153

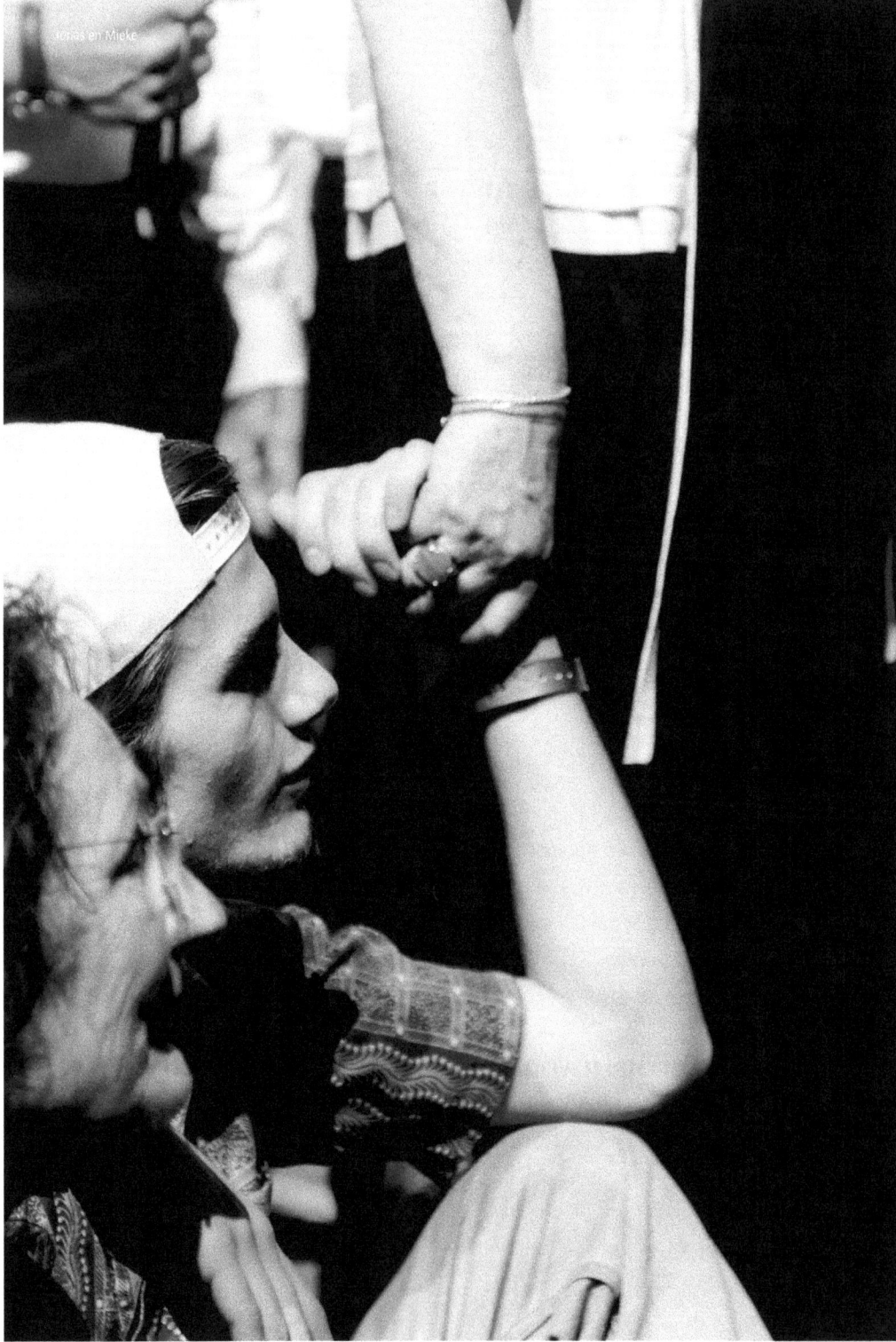
Jonas en Mieke

INTRODUCTION

1. We Are All Included

Ger Tielen

Age Segregation

Age segregation seems to be hard to eradicate. The Grimm Brothers' fairy tale "The Old Man and his Grandson" illustrated the predicament of people who have grown old and vulnerable:

There was once a very old man, whose eyes had become dim, his ears dull of hearing, his knees trembled, and when he sat at the table he could hardly hold the spoon, and spilt the broth upon the table-cloth or let it run out of his mouth. His son and his son's wife were disgusted at this, so the old grandfather at last had to sit in the corner behind the stove. They gave him his food, and not even enough of it, in a wooden bowl so that he would not break the earthenware. One day, the little grandson of four years old began to gather together some bits of wood upon the ground. "What are you doing there?" asked the father. "I am making a little trough," answered the child, "for father and mother to eat out of when I am big." The man and his wife looked at each other, and deeply ashamed, they took the old grandfather back to the table, and henceforth always let him eat with them, and likewise said nothing if he did spill a little of anything.

In spite of the best intentions, with the expansion of the welfare state, age segregation took on an institutional dimension in the care of older people. In 1990, in the Netherlands, seven per cent of the population over 65 lived in an old people's home or care centre. Living in these facilities may not be as extreme as in the "no kids allowed" Suncities into which well-to-do older people withdraw in the USA, but nonetheless, it can be regarded as a mild form of segregation. Only now that the institutionalisation of so many older people has become too big a financial burden, do we enter a new phase. Currently, elderly people are encouraged to remain living in their own homes with the support of family, friends, and neighbours in the local community.

The oscillation between segregation and integration can also be seen in other sectors. In the 1980s, large numbers of people over 55 exited the labour market, assisted by various early-retirement schemes. This accounted both for jobs in businesses and governmental institutions. The percentage of 55- to 64-year-old men in paid employment decreased during that period from 80 to 27 percent in 1993. The rationale was that older people would make way for the younger generation for whom job opportunities were bleak. Such substitution is also a form of segregation. Moreover, not only were the retirement schemes in vain, the younger generation still faced unemployment, and by the end of the century, it had become clear that these schemes were too expensive to keep up. The introduction of the Anti-Age-Discrimination Act of 2004, the raising of the retirement age to 67, and the introduction of diversity policies for businesses resulted in an increase in the number of older people in paid employment to almost 70 per cent of 55- to 64-year-old men. That is what I call a great act of integration.

A similar swing from segregation to integration is discernible in the Dutch media. In the 1980s, older people began to disappear from the television screen, and there was less and less space for older people in the press, fashion, and commercials. This can be interpreted as a direct outcome of the generational conflicts of the 1960s: the baby boomers, who were by then in charge, were fixated on remaining young and dynamic. Older models, actors, and above all, actresses were put out of work. Here too, the turn of the century signalled the beginning of a new phase. Although the faces and voices of older people are increasingly seen and heard in the media, simultaneously a new form of segregation emerges. PLUS magazine and broadcasting corporation Omroep MAX, both catering specifically to the older generation, are highly successful in the Netherlands. MAX' programmes have even replaced Sesame Street at the hour and broadcasting channel Dutch children have been watching it for decades.

This brief account tells us that the oscillation between segregation and integration is apparently unlikely to reach a permanent equilibrium. Where some forms of segregation disappear, others emerge. These developments express a strong financial motivation to fight age segregation. But surely, there are more pressing reasons to eradicate it. As a society, we need to work continuously toward the prevention of age discrimination and other forms of discrimination in all societal domains. We should strive for a permanent dialogue and collaboration between people of all different generations in social, cultural, and political organisations and institutions. Why? Because of societal urgencies and because of its positive outcomes. There is a need to stimulate relations between generations, because generational and historical awareness enables people to invest in each other.

Specifically in a time in which our government hands over its responsibility for care, welfare, and the social domain to citizens, reciprocity is key.

Generations and Diversity

There are several examples of intergenerational approaches that yield positive outcomes. Experiences with diversity management in business show that intergenerational (and intercultural) collaboration improves productivity. Generations differ from one another in the possibilities offered by the times in which they grew up. The media, music, and technologies of an era define the experience of a generation, in addition to the shifting parental educational norms. Social work based on such generational awareness unleashes—so is the experience—unexpected creative and innovative forces with many possibilities for action. Similar experiences were identified in discussions following the viewing of films with intergenerational storylines. In MusicGenerations, the intergenerational music programme that is central to this volume, the energy set free in the collaboration between older and younger talents is tremendous. Moreover, the programme shows how much the generations enjoy working together. It is simply fun!

Acknowledging age diversity is important, but does not suffice. Our societies are increasingly super-diverse and large numbers of people continue to migrate to Europe and North America. Besides working toward the prevention of age discrimination, as a society, we need to work toward the eradication of other forms of discrimination as well. We also need to realise that working from an intergenerational awareness is inevitably to work from an intercultural—super-diverse—perspective (and vice versa). It is such messages that practices such as MusicGenerations convey, and make them valuable and worth studying. Both the philosophy and the approach underpinning such practices may also carry some of the answers to questions currently raised by the arrival of large numbers of refugees and their integration into our Western societies.

> Besides working toward the prevention of age discrimination, as a society, we need to work toward the eradication of other forms of discrimination as well.

MusicGenerations

MusicGenerations began as a song contest for migrant seniors, called the Euro+ Songfestival, during the celebrations of Cultural Capital of Europe in the Dutch city of Rotterdam in 2001. In subsequent years, the music programme evolved into a musical encounter between generations under the name MusicGenerations - Appendix I provides some facts and figures. This on-going programme connects young people between 14 and 25 years, and people over 50 through music, including rap, hip hop, poetry en spoken word.

The talents enter a series of master classes, workshops, and rehearsals. As a group, they work toward concerts at festivals and a range of cultural venues. The composition of the group is diverse in terms of age, of ethnic, cultural, and socio-economic backgrounds, and in musical taste. The programme carefully combines talent development, reciprocity between ages and cultures, and urgent social issues. By changing the theme of the programme periodically, the MusicGenerations' organisation responds to and expresses its involvement in political issues, such as the alienation between generations, the celebration of 70 years of freedom since World War II in 2015, or the present-day arrival of refugees.

> The programme carefully combines talent development, reciprocity between ages and cultures, and urgent social issues.

MusicGenerations is rooted in the strong conviction that the arts can and should function as a meeting place. It understands artists as experts in dealing with uncertainty and arts projects as spaces for ambiguity. The collective lingering in such spaces may result in a deeper understanding of what otherwise remains just hype or a trend. This is a valuable contribution in a time in which digital forums, news broadcasts, and political debates are jam-packed with one-dimensional statements made by people who nonetheless all claim to know the truth. The one-dimensionality, the half-truths, and the lack of genuine dialogue fall short of dismantling the man-made complexity and hampers society from moving in more progressive directions.

The Background of this Volume

In this volume, two developments converge. First, this volume compiles the insights of a one-day conference in October 2015. At this conference, the foundation behind MusicGenerations, Stichting Euro+Songfestival, shared its 15 years of experience in working with the arts, age, and diversity. The conference aimed at stimulating critical reflection on these themes and on present-day forms of exclusion. The presentations of the keynote speakers, the moderator, and the workshop leaders at the conference, provided the basis of their contributions to this volume (chapters 5, 6, 8, and 9). Their various roles at the conference are reflected in their contributions, in terms of length and style. Some contributions are more scholarly, others more column-like. Here too, we preferred difference to uniformity! See Appendix II for more information on both the authors and their role in de conference.

Second, this volume is based on the insights provided by a research project organised around MusicGenerations' 2015 programme "Talent for Freedom." Stichting Euro+Songfestival commissioned the research, which was conducted by Sandra Trienekens, who was assisted with different stages of the research by Milda Saltenyte and Britt Swartjes. Chapters 2, 4, 7 and 10 are particularly rooted in this research trajectory. In this research project, MusicGenerations' development of musical programmes was read against the backdrop of Dutch integration policy discourses and cultural policy's approach to cultural diversity in the arts. A video-analysis was made of

"Now or Never," MusicGenerations' previous programme, and of comparable music projects dealing with age. Additionally, fieldwork was conducted during the Talent for Freedom programme. The fieldwork consisted of observations of the rehearsals and concerts in Rotterdam and Amsterdam in spring 2015; of interviews with the MusicGenerations team and a selection of the participants; and of a questionnaire that was completed by a total of 39 participants. The audiences were approached with a "quick and dirty" version of the most significant change method.

The Contributions

The contributions to this volume predominantly refer to developments in Dutch policies, political developments, and public debates. As such, this volume offers insight into the specific case of the Netherlands as a site for inclusion.

Central to Part I is the question of how art, and in particular music, contributes to social and political issues around age and intergenerationality, diversity, and freedom. Starting from actual artistic practices, the questions addressed are: What art initiatives can be discerned and what do we learn from them (chapter 2)? From there, we focus on the elements in the MusicGenerations' approach that can be more widely adapted to cultural and other interventions aimed at bridging among people from a wide range of backgrounds (chapter 4). In chapter 5, taking up the question of how the artistic approach (methodology) can be an inspiration to non-arts sectors, Marjolein Gysels addresses practices that involve people with Alzheimer's disease. She explores how artists let the voices of these people be heard and how their voices can even become part of research into dementia. Chapter 6, the concluding chapter of this part, adopts a meta-perspective on the power of the arts. By borrowing from neurobiology, psychology, and sociology, Eltje Bos analyses the power of the arts—and specifically music—for individuals, groups, and society.

Central to Part II is the question of what inclusion entails nowadays. In chapter 7, the progressively inclusive experiences of 15 years of MusicGenerations are juxtaposed with the increasingly exclusionary discourses on "cultural diversity" in cultural and integration polices and in public debates. How to enhance both the vocabulary and our understanding of diversity in our contemporary society? In chapter 8 Zihni Özdil wonders if "mixing," physically, and also mentally, would be an appropriate perspective for post-multicultural Dutch citizenship. He questions our inclination to assume that diversity or difference and mixing contradict each other. In chapter 9, Maurice Crul discusses how the concept of super-diversity can help advance our understanding of (theories of) assimilation and integration. Crul concludes that super-diversity theory offers an intersectional approach as a way ahead, but that the integration context too is crucial in explaining processes of successful inclusion. Özdil and Crul offer important insights in a time in which European societies such as the Netherlands fear further fragmentation of society and polarization between societal groups. Social cohesion policy is thought able to right such wrongs. In chapter 10, by contrasting popular assumptions underpinning the concept of social cohesion to the "small realities" observable in the Music Generations' Talent for Freedom programme, Sandra Trienekens further extends Özdil's and Crul's search for a post-multicultural approach to inclusion and new Dutch citizenship. How can the reality, presented by a music project such as MusicGenerations' Talent for Freedom, be an example for an inclusive society?

The volume concludes with the implications for policy, funding, and education, e.g., social work. What do the different perspectives presented in this volume articulate with regard to how policy and funding programmes are set up and how we can best teach our students intergenerational and post-multicultural awareness?

Conny Groot

PART I

MUSIC, AGE AND DIVERSITY

2. Art Projects on Age and Diversity

Sandra Trienekens & Britt Swartjes

MusicGenerations is an intergenerational program for talent development. It started by working with first generation migrant seniors, in the programme "Euro+ Songfestival" during Rotterdam Cultural Capital of Europe in 2001. Later on, the music director selected and arranged the songs in such a way that dialogue between the music preferences of the various generations and cultures as well as between the participating talents themselves were triggered. Since then, the composition of the group of talents has become diverse in terms of age, ethnic, cultural, and socio-economic backgrounds, and in musical taste. Every new edition of the programme is dedicated to talent development and to a carefully selected theme, which allows for reciprocity between generations and cultures and which addresses a pressing social issue. An example is the "Talent for Freedom" programme, which took place from 2014 to 2015 and referenced Europe's commemoration of the end of World War II. "Talent for Freedom" thus evolved around the themes of age, generations, diversity, music, and the meaning of freedom to different people.

MusicGenerations does not stand alone in its quest for inclusion. There are other national and international culture and arts initiatives that work around one or more of these themes. This chapter provides a brief overview and places the practice of MusicGenerations against the backdrop of other comparable programmes. The examples were chosen because of their inspiring nature and the enthusiastic responses they trigger in their audiences. Eclectic as the collection of examples may appear, it shows us at least three things. First, there is a variety of ways in which the arts are and can be used to bring together people from different ages, ethnic, and cultural backgrounds. There is no one format that fits all. Second, even a brief insight into the initiatives reveals several similarities in the way the initiatives are set up. Lessons can be drawn for future initiatives. Third, the overview shows the strength of MusicGenerations multidimensional approach—dealing with all themes simultaneously—and as such, it functions as a rationale for the study of Talent for Freedom.

Art and Age

As a response to the aging populations and changing demographics of contemporary European societies, older people receive quite a lot of policy attention in individual European countries and from the European Commission. In the Netherlands, the focus on seniors is further strengthened by the decentralisation of care and welfare policies to the community level. One thing that one notices is that many initiatives start from a one-dimensional approach. They target only or predominantly seniors, as is the case with the majority of (European) Life Long Learning programmes as well as with the majority of projects supported by the Dutch Long Live Art programme which promotes cultural participation among older people on the basis of its beneficial effects on people's well-being (see Hortulanus, Jonkers, & Stuyvers, 2012).

Although these projects often fail to take up the opportunity to connect seniors to other age groups, there are several inspiring examples of cultural projects. There is, for instance, a cultural route for lonely elderly people, called "Route 65 Plus," in which they can participate in all kinds of (digital) cultural activities (www.langlevekunst.nl, 2016a). Another example is the program "Parels voor de Kunst" (Pearls for the Art) (www.langlevekunst.nl, 2016b). Here, elderly people have the opportunity to sign up for, for example, dance or story writing. Even though it is not the main focus of the Long Live Art programme, some projects do indeed connect younger and older people. One example is a project in which children and elderly people form an intergenerational orchestra (www.langlevekunst.nl, 2016c). In these projects, age, generations, and different forms of art are connected to the theme of well-being, and above all, tend to express the message of the importance of cultural participation by elderly people. If the themes of diversity or freedom play a role at all, it is in a rather indirect manner.

> In these projects, age, generations, and different forms of art are connected to the theme of well-being, and above all, tend to express the message of the importance of cultural participation by elderly people.

Art, Age, and Vitality

There are also art projects that deal specifically with age, but move beyond the level of mere participation to convey a strong message to society at large: that being old does not equal being boring or uninteresting! One example is the Young at Heart Chorus based in Northampton, Massachusetts. This endearing music project revolving around seniors was an inspiration to MusicGenerations. The restructuring effect on representation made an especially deep impression. At the beginning of a Young at Heart concert, one sees just a group of older people on stage: at the end, the group has "decomposed" into individuals and one has gotten to meet all their different qualities.

A 100-minute documentary *Young@Heart*, directed by Stephen Walker and Sally George in 2007, provides great insight into this chorus of singers. The average age is 81 and many singers must overcome health issues to participate. Although they have toured the world and sung for royalty, the documentary focuses on rehearsals for a concert in their hometown, which succeeds in spite of several really heart breaking events such as the passing away of co-singers. What is so captivating about this documentary is the behaviour of the seniors. If the connotation of "old age" is lack of energy and passivity, the seniors in this choir prove the exact opposite. Singing songs by artists such as James Brown and Sonic Youth, they are portrayed as full of energy, drive, action, and cheerfulness. At concerts, audiences go mental as a consequence. Here the category "old" acquires unexpected qualities: being wild, energetic, creative, and vital—qualities commonly associated with youth. This example from the other side of the Atlantic carries a message similar to that of MusicGenerations: singing and passion for music are at the very core and are presented as a way of staying alive, as a drive for life. Additionally, seniors are portrayed as vital and talented. On the other hand, the Young at Heart Chorus does not pick up intergenerationality and diversity as themes. When they performed in a prison for inmates, the theme of freedom was indeed addressed, albeit indirectly.

A Dutch art project stemming from the vitality of older people is "Peptide, Portretten van Oma's" (Peptide, Portraits of Grandmothers). This is a theatrical performance by Saskia Meulendijks (Studio La Meul) about the lives of twelve grandmothers with international roots or intercultural experiences. By relating their stories to the audience, Meulendijks seeks to break through stereotypical images of grandmothers in general, and specifically, of grandmothers with transnational bonds. The process started with elderly people being trained in the writing and telling of stories. Next, Meulendijks interviewed a selection of grandmothers extensively and compiled their life experiences into a coherent performance. During the performance, the stories were supported by the projection of photographs of the grandmothers in the different phases of their lives and by three musicians playing live music inspired by songs that meant something to the grandmothers (Trienekens, 2011). Diversity, or in this case transnationality, was at the core of this project. Indirectly, the stories of the grandmothers reiterated personal struggles for freedom and self-definition. The project also made an interesting point about age, for some of the grandmas were still very young. Intergenerationality, however, was not an explicit goal.

Art, Age, and Care

In our research into art projects on age, we were struck by the number of initiatives that focus on care. An example of this is "Onvergetelijk van Abbe" (Unforgettable van Abbe), which is designed for people with Alzheimer's disease. The Stedelijk Museum Amsterdam and the Van Abbemuseum were inspired by the MoMa programme of the Museum of Modern Art in New York. The programme consists of interactive tours of the museums. It is based on the idea that looking at art gives people with dementia the opportunity to exchange ideas, without having to fall back on their short-term memory (www.vanabbemuseum.nl, 2016).

Other art initiatives bring together different generations, but they too are often set up around care or welfare, aiming at enhancing or increasing solidarity. Far fewer programmes around arts and culture allow the generations to meet as equally talented people and are aimed at letting them have fun together. The EU hosts several initiatives promoting intergenerational dialogue and cooperation. For instance, EAGLE (European Approaches to Inter-Generational Lifelong Learning) is a European cooperation project, which aims at exploring learning opportunities between different generations, within the concept of Lifelong Learning. Additionally, the AGE Platform Europe is a network that involves more than 150 organizations and works toward creating and raising awareness of the importance of cooperation and solidarity between generations. The platform actively promotes EU Day on Intergenerational Solidarity, on April 29 annually. Both platforms list and describe best practices, the majority of which are social in nature and aimed at care, welfare, education, or the labour market. One example is the German federal model of *Mehrgenerationenhäuser* (multigenerational houses). These "drop-in" community centres function as open meeting places for people of different age groups in a specific community or city, where mutual exchange takes place around specific needs (care, mentoring, homework assistance, childcare—see: EAGLE 2007a). Another example is the Belgian cohabitation program that connects students looking for accommodation and elderly people living alone and in need of company (EAGLE 2007b). Only a few examples involve the arts, such as The Actors House, Romania, and the Les Deux Mémoires organization dedicated to generating intergenerational collaboration through film.

In the Netherlands too, we find several art projects focused on generations that are set up around care or welfare. For example, Zona's kiosk is a traveling platform with art for elderly people in nursing homes. It has set up multiple projects in which children are involved. One example is the project "Weesbeesten" (Orphaned Animals), which focuses on art and dementia. The idea is that children write a sad story about a decrepit stuffed animal that has apparently gotten lost. The elderly person then adopts the stuffed animal, and together with the children, the animal is given a bed or nest (www.zonaskiosk.nl, 2016). "Kijk in mijn ogen" (Look into my Eyes) by Pra Muziektheater is another example of a project that involves occupants of nursing homes. Children and elderly people work together on a diptych for a year with dancers, writers, musicians, a choreographer, and a stage-manager. The themes are displacement, contact, and feeling safe.

> Eventually, the generations perform together in a dance presentation, in which the contact between elderly people and children is emphasized.

Eventually, the generations perform together in a dance presentation, in which the contact between elderly people and children is emphasized. One of the occupants of the nursing home stated, "It was just like therapy, but fun!" The children also enjoyed dancing with the elderly people and enjoyed seeing how much fun they had (www.cultuurparticipatie.nl, 2016).

An inspiring intergenerational art project that does not focus on care is "Twee keer Kijken" (Look Twice). This project is initiated by Foam, the Amsterdam museum of photography, and the idea is that elderly people and youngsters regularly take photographs together over a period of five weeks. Through this project, Foam sought to discover which dynamics and creativity arise when generations experience new things with each other. Taking photographs is thought to be an accessible way to start a conversation, and by working on photography assignments, one begins to see the perspective of the other generation (www.foam.org, 2016). The project takes place in Amsterdam, and although it does not explicitly focus on diversity in ethnic backgrounds, the younger people often are of different backgrounds than the elderly people. Freedom does not function as a theme in this project.

Art and Diversity

A music project that focuses on diversity, rather than on age, is "Orchestre Partout." This orchestra consists of refugees who play music from their countries of origin and perform at festivals and in asylum seeker centres (www.5ekwartier.nl, 2016). The purpose of this project is to show the diversity of music and the skills and competences of the (ex) refugees who are marginalised by society. The project tries to deal with the designation of minorities as "others." The founder of the project, Ted van Leeuwen (5e Kwartier), uses dramaturgy and personal stories of the band members to ensure that the audience gets to know the people behind the music. In this way, the audience is able to understand the narratives (Van Heugten, 2014). The audience is indeed affected by the music. People applaud enthusiastically when they hear a song from their country, and when a sensitive song is played, even some noisy men become silent (Van der Valk, 2012). With regard to the musicians, Van der Valk (2012) shows that a sense of mutual trust is created within the band, so that all these people from different countries can play music together harmoniously. Even though they don't speak the same language, the musicians express a better understanding of each other through making music together (van der Valk, 2012). As this project primarily aims at bringing together people from different countries and the creation of mutual understanding between them through the power of music, diversity is at its the core.

An example of project by 5e Kwartier that focuses on both diversity and intergenerationality is "Rent a Granny," directed by Titia Bouwmeester in collaboration with Don't Hit Mama. In this project, young and elderly people exchanged stories, music and, dance in a performance. Questions such as "What is home?" and "Who am I in relation to others?" were addressed. Elderly people told the youngsters how their identity was formed when they emigrated at a young age. They detailed their lives in-between two worlds and the tension between their acquired and ascribed identities. The youngsters mirrored themselves in the stories and were invited to scrutinize their own lives. Bridging differences in age and ethnic backgrounds sometimes proved difficult (Bouwmeester in Trienekens 2006). Therefore, in the process, the focus was put on creation of trust. 5e Kwartier provided a safe, receptive environment in which the generations could have fun together. The creation of communality was one of the goals of this project. Freedom was not an explicit theme, but just like the stories of the grandmas in Peptide, some of the stories were indeed tales of the struggle for personal freedom and self-definition.

> Elderly people told the youngsters how their identity was formed when they emigrated at a young age.

Art, War, and Freedom

"Talent for Freedom" added another theme to the approach of MusicGenerations: freedom. It explored the common striving for freedom and what freedom means to different people. Another Dutch art project that focuses on the concept of freedom and intergenerationality is "Oorlog in mijn Buurt" (War in my Neighbourhood). Since 2012, this project has brought together older people and primary school children through story telling in the various boroughs of Amsterdam. The children interview elderly people who lived in their neighbourhoods during World War II. The children then present the war stories of the older people, and consequently, become the new storytellers of the history of their neighbourhood (www.oorloginmijnbuurt.nl, 2016). The goal of this project is the creation of a shared past, the participation of youngsters in the community (historical awareness), and the enrichment of the school curriculum. By emphasizing the transfer of war stories of elderly people to youngsters, the concept of freedom and the differences in the meaning of freedom for the different generations, become evident. Given the myriad of ethnic backgrounds of the youngsters, this project indirectly deals with diversity.

> The children interview elderly people who lived in their neighbourhoods during World War II.

Another Dutch art initiative addressing freedom is "Song of Survival" by Malle Babbe, an all-women's choir from the city of Haarlem. Two women, who were imprisoned in Japanese internment camps during World War II, composed the songs. They based their work on what survived of the songs women in the camps sang together, putting together what they could remember of the classical music scores they loved to listen to or play before the war. Helen Colijn, one of the survivors of the camp, wrote a book about her experiences and the songs (Colijn, 1989). Inspired by this book, Malle Babbe performed "Song of Survival" for the first time in 1989. The choir still performs this work at commemorations and concerts (www.vrouwenkoormallebabbe.nl, 2016). In 1997, the book was turned into a film called Paradise Road, directed by Bruce Beresford.

"Syrious Mission" is a musical project around present-day war and lack of freedom. Dutch composer Merlijn Twaalfhoven created this initiative for children in Syrian refugee camps in Jordan. Musicians volunteer to give workshops, collect money for instruments, and prepare the children for the concerts they give in the camps (www.wijblijvenhier.nl, 2016). Another musical program dealing with present-day conflict is the "West-Eastern Divan Orchestra," in which Arab and Israeli musicians collaborate. As such, the orchestra defies strong political divides in the Middle East. Edward W. Said and Daniel Barenboim founded the orchestra when they realized the need for an alternative way to address the Israeli-Palestinian conflict. Although the musicians do not always agree on politics, there is a sense of mutual respect. The goal of the project is reflected in the statement of the orchestra: "We aspire to total freedom and equality between Israelis and Palestinians, and it is on this basis that we come together today to play music" (www.west-eastern-divan.org, 2016). Here, diversity and freedom are both an important focus.

The Power of Music

We chose examples from the various artistic disciplines to illustrate the wide range of projects that use the power of the arts for issues around age, diversity, and/or freedom. MusicGenerations positively exploits the power of *music*: music making and singing speak to the heart and empower people.

Active cultural participation in music also appears to have certain benefits for older and younger people. Earlier research has shown that music offers powerful ways for enhancing health and well-being in old age. Making music has been found to provide a source of enhanced social cohesion, enjoyment, personal development, and empowerment (Coffman, 2002; Sixsmith & Gibson, 2007). There also is some evidence of the social and emotional value for elderly people who participate in intergenerational group music activities (Bowers, 1998; Darrow, Johnson, & Ollenberger, 1994). Wide benefits of music for younger people are well documented as well (Hallam, 2010).
MusicGenerations' previous programme "Now or Never" was set up around personal empowerment and well-being. It aimed at making its audiences aware of the urgency of intergenerational dialogue. "Talent for Freedom" takes a political stance and conveys the message of "a vision of a diverse, caring society." It aims at restructuring popular

stereotypical images of both old people and our super-diverse societies, and at drawing our attention to the need to collectively safeguard our freedom.

The power of protest songs has been manifest in most historic eras. It is largely from this musical genre that "Talent for Freedom" drew its set list. The participants performed songs such as "Cambia" (Mercedes Sosa) and "Redemption Song" (Bob Marley), but also more recent Kurdish and Armenian songs of freedom. In his talk, preceding the Amsterdam premiere of the Talent for Freedom concert, musicologist Anton Snijders brought to mind the effect songs such as Stevie Wonder's 1974 "You Haven't Done Nothin'" (against Nixon), Fela Kuti's 1977 "Zombie" (against the Nigerian regime), or Peter Gabriel's 1980 "Biko" (against apartheid in South-Africa) had at the time. Snijders argues that contemporary protest songs sound differently and we will have to learn how to recognize them. For instance, he understands certain rap songs as protest songs. The Talent for Freedom workshops were indeed given by Dutch rap stars such as Blaxtar and Yes-R, both known for their critical analysis of Dutch political and public debates on integration in their lyrics.

The protest songs on the set list of MusicGenerations' Talent for Freedom concerts go down well with the participants. They may not all be fond of every song, but they all adhere to the message of freedom. One older Indonesian-Dutch woman wonders, "What have I been listening to all my life? These songs carry an important message. I no longer want to listen to songs solely about love or the loss thereof!" An older Dutch-Dutch woman with roots in the women emancipation movement of the 1960s and 1970s is glad for a different reason: "Finally, we can sing protest songs again. And, apparently, even the younger generation is getting interested!" But above all, it is the singing that unites the group; what they all have in common is a strong passion for music and singing.

> "Finally, we can sing protest songs again. And, apparently, even the younger generation is getting interested!"

In Short

We have presented only a handful of projects taken from Dutch and international contexts. The aim was not to give a meticulous overview, but a taste of the wide range of initiatives by musicians and other artists working on age, generations, diversity, and/or freedom. Were we to draw conclusions from this overview, we would come up with these two:

In spite of their vast differences, the art projects described, have several elements in common: they use the power of music or the arts to make space for people to have fun and enjoy their interaction. They work on the creation of trust and a positive environment for their participants, where joy and creative collaboration can become manifest. The identities of the people involved and/or their stories are the central point, and are shared with other participants and the audiences. And, one way or another, the messages these projects convey reconstruct stereotypes of older people and/or migrants. The projects highlight "hidden" elements of their characters—that is, largely hidden for the outside world.

The reading of MusicGenerations against other initiatives also exemplifies why the MusicGenerations programme "Talent for Freedom" is worth studying. We have seen that MusicGenerations is not unique in addressing the themes of age, generations, diversity, or freedom. What is unique is its multidimensional focus on all of these themes simultaneously. Its strength is its multi-dimensional message. Not only does Talent for Freedom convey the message that old people are fun, charming, talented, and can be extremely vital. It simultaneously speaks of (super)diversity, places age in an intergenerational context, and shows multiple interpretations of the concept of freedom as well as the connecting power of shared concepts such as passion for music and singing. The next chapters provide us with the details.

References

Bowers, J. (1998). Effects of an intergenerational choir for community-based seniors and college students on age-related attitudes. *Journal of Music Therapy, 35*(1), 2–18.

Colijn, H. (1989). *De kracht van een lied: Overleven in een vrouwenkamp.* Uitgever: Uitgeverij Van Wijnen.

Coffman, D. D. (2002). Music and quality of life in older adults. *Psychomusicology, 18*(1-2), 76–88.

Darrow, A. A., Johnson, C. M., & Ollenberger, T. (1994). The effect of participation in an intergenerational choir on teens' and older persons' cross age attitudes. *Journal of Music Therapy, 31*(2), 119–134.

EAGLE. (2007a). *Multigenerational House Nürnberg, Germany: Case Study*; Authors: S. Heid & A. Liebenberg. FIM-NewLearning, University of Erlangen-Nuremberg. http://www.globalaging.org/elderrights/world/2007/multigenerational07.pdf

EAGLE. (2007b). *Intergenerational practices in Europe: Field Research Synthesis Report.* Authors: N. Zygouritsas. FIM-NewLearning, University of Erlangen-Nuremberg. http://www.eagle-project.eu/welcome-to-eagle/practice-showcase

Hallam, S. (2010). The power of music: Its impact on the intellectual, personal and social development of children and young people. *International Journal of Music Education, 38*(3), 269–289.

Hortulanus, R., Jonkers, M., & Stuyvers, D. (2012). *Kunstbeoefening met ambitie. Naar een lokaal stimulerings en facilteringsprogramma voor kunstbeoefening door ouderen.* LESI Rapporten 2012/07. Utrecht: Landelijk Expertisecentrum Sociale Interventie.

Sixsmith, A., & Gibson, G. (2007). Music and the well-being of people with dementia. *Ageing & Society, 27*(1), 127–145.

Trienekens, S. (2006). *Kunst en sociaal engagement. Een analyse van de relatie tussen kunst, de wijk en de gemeenschap.* http://www.lkca.nl/~/media/downloads/ws_2006_ce_17.pdf

Trienekens, S. (2011). *Wrikken aan beeldvorming. Vier community art-projecten, vier verhalen.* Rotterdam: Kosmopolis.

Van der Valk, L. (2012). *De band van gevluchte muzikanten.* Obtained on 2 February 2016 from: http://www.leendertvandervalk.nl/NRC_Handelsblad_en_nrc.next_files/orchestre%20partout.pdf

Van Heugten, L. (2014). Tuning in to European dissonance. In A. Lengyel (Ed.). *Karaoke Europe: A handbook to social specific theatre* (pp. 98–115). http://hdl.handle.net/11245/1.431703

Websites Consulted

www.5ekwartier.nl (2016). *Orchestre Partout, band zonder verblijfsvergunning.* Retrieved on 3 February 2016: http://www.5ekwartier.nl/archief/orchestre-partout/karaoke-europe-orchestre-partout-winterconcerten/

www.cultuurparticipatie.nl (2016). Consulted on 3 February 2016 via: http://www.cultuurparticipatie.nl/subsidies/ouderenparticipatie/gehonoreerde-projecten/kijk-in-mijn-ogen-358.html

www.foam.org (2016). Consulted on 2 February 2016 via: http://www.foam.org/nl/over-ons/press-office/twee-keer-kijken

www.langlevedekunst.nl (2016a). Consulted on 4 February 2016 via: http://www.langlevekunst.nl/nieuws/route-65-plus-voor-eenzame-ouderen/

www.langlevedekunst.nl (2016b). Consulted on 4 February 2016 via: http://www.langlevekunst.nl/nieuws/nieuw-kunst-en-cultuurprogramma-voor-60-parels-voor-de-kunst/

www.langlevedekunst.nl (2016c). Consulted on 4 February 2016 via: http://www.langlevekunst.nl/nieuws/zwolse-scholieren-en-ouderen-samen-in-een-orkest/

www.oorloginmijnbuurt.nl (2016). Consulted on 4 February 2016 via: http://www.oorloginmijnbuurt.nl/over-oorlog-in-mijn-buurt/

www.vanabbemuseum.nl (2016). Consulted on 3 February 2016 via: http://vanabbemuseum.nl/het-museum/educatie/special-guests/alzheimer-programma/

www.vrouwenkoormallebabe.nl (2016). Consulted on 4 February 2016 via: http://www.vrouwenkoor-mallebabbe.nl/song.html

www.west-eastern-divan.org (2016). Consulted on 4 February 2016 via: http://www.west-eastern-divan.org/

www.wijblijvenhier.nl (2016). Consulted on 4 February 2016 via: https://wijblijvenhier.nl/21575/syrious-mission-muziek-maken-vluchtelingenkampen/

Zena, Mirik, Ferry, Jonas and Wouter

3. Age Ain't Nothin' But a Number

Conny Groot

Age ain't nothing but a number, throwing down ain't nothing but a thing, This loving I have for you it'll never change.

<small>Age Ain't Nothing But a Number, song by Aaliyah</small>

The recognition of seniors as valuable carriers of cultural heritage occurred to me more or less accidently. After graduating from Theatre Studies at the advanced age of 40, I started working for Cinekid, the Dutch children's film and television festival. But then, fate stepped in. The Dutch counterpart of the Irish-British "Images of Aging" festival was looking for a programmer and they were looking my way.

Back in 1998, images of seniors in film, television, and photography were still quite novel. The baby boomers, who were in charge of most of our image factories, had already decided in the sixties that they would never age: "Live hard, die young." In such an era, seeing so many movies featuring seniors made me aware of how fragmented the portrayal of this large part of the world population is. Remembering and honouring my own grandparents, who were the most loving and courageous people, was quite a saddening awareness since the Netherlands is indebted to its seniors for the complete reconstruction of the country after World War II.

<small>Someone once said that ageing may be the biggest challenge to the West since World War II.</small>

Someone once said that ageing may be the biggest challenge to the West since World War II. Never in the history of mankind have there been so many—relatively well-to-do—seniors. How will that number change our culture, our housing and city development, our care and transportation systems? We are not even halfway toward finding out. But we will all be confronted with the need to create opportunities to recognize people over 50 for their contributions to society. Each person will do so from his or her own talents. Mine are limited to arts and culture. In my experience, working with seniors and the different generations in film, music, and debate has been nothing but a privilege.

The joke we made during the Euro+ Songfestival programme in 2001, "First we take the senior homes, then we take the world," became true. Our programmes with the talented generations have taken us all over Europe, Turkey, Kurdistan, and the United States. The generosity of our participants and sponsors has enabled us to challenge our young and senior talents, and most of all, ourselves. "Be the best you can be" inspires all involved to make room for the talented of heart and voice. A great example, and an inspiration to our programmes, is the work of the Young @ Heart Chorus. In their concerts, they alternate between group pieces for the truly dedicated and solo pieces for the truly great. Our music director Paul Mayer (musician and psychologist) achieves a comparable quality through his absolute love for music and our talents. He masters the fine art of finding just the right place, for just the right talent, in just the right crossover composition.

That leaves me with nothing but gratitude for the generations that have joined our programme with their talents. Some of them have been with us from the beginning in 2001. Together, they convey the message of a caring, inclusive society. Through our combined talents, we are ready to address the next pressing social issue through our music. I am also grateful to our sponsors. Most of them have supported and trusted us since the very beginning, acknowledging that ageing may be a challenge, but in the end, "age ain't nothing but a number."

4. Getting to Know MusicGenerations

Sandra Trienekens & Milda Saltenyte

In the tradition of discourse analysis, we read MusicGenerations' music programmes as text and its messages and restructuring effects as social practice in this chapter. We adopt Jørgensen and Phillips' (2002, p.80) approach, based on Fairclough's 1995 three-dimensional model for critical discourse analysis. The three dimensions are text, *discursive practice* and social practice.

The analysis of text generally focuses on speech, writing, visual images, or a combination of these. In the case of MusicGenerations, we understand "text" as the overall image the music programmes produce: the people involved, the repertoire of songs, the stage image, and the programme's message. We will read two of MusicGenerations' music programmes as texts: "Now or Never" and "Talent for Freedom." Both programmes were produced by Conny Groot in close collaboration with MusicGenerations' music director Paul Mayer.

MusicGenerations brings about a particular understanding and representation of social reality by embracing and promoting a vision of an inclusive and caring society. Both the repertoire and mix of people singing together on stage convey a message to the audience and the wider world. The practices and messages that MusicGenerations creates are embedded in discourse(s), and in turn, contribute to their (re)production. This discursive practice is central to chapter 7, in which 15 years of MusicGenerations is read against the developments in Dutch cultural and integration policy.

Such discursive practices not only contribute to the reproduction of an already existing structure, but also can challenge and restructure the existing order of discourse by using different words and meanings, which refer to what may lie outside the structure (Fairclough, 1992b, p. 66: cited in Jørgensen & Phillips, 2002, p. 65). Participatory arts practices can indeed have a transformative effect (cf. Trienekens & Hillaert, 2015) and thus have consequences for the broader social practice. Chapter 7 and 10 explore the wider implications; in this chapter, we analyse the extent to which "Talent for Freedom" has had a restructuring effect on its participants and audiences.

The information for this chapter is derived from video-analysis of "Now or Never," and from fieldwork in the case of "Talent for freedom." The fieldwork consisted of structured observations of rehearsals and concerts in Rotterdam and Amsterdam in spring 2015, of interviews with the MusicGenerations team and a selection of the participants, and of a questionnaire that was completed by 39 of the participants. The audiences were approached with a "quick and dirty" version of the most significant change method and were asked for the strongest change in perspective after watching the concert.

This chapter's reading of MusicGenerations serves several goals. First, it allows us to get to know MusicGenerations and its programmes. Second, it shows "Talent for Freedom's" (tentative) restructuring effect on the participants and the audiences. Third, the account of the MusicGenerations programmes provides insight into MusicGenerations' specific approach—extending the list of effective elements in the artistic working method of the art programmes presented in chapter 2.

MusicGenerations' Programmes as Text

In the case of MusicGenerations, we understand "text" as the overall image the music programmes produce: the people involved, the repertoire of songs, the stage image, and the programme's message. The themes and set-up of the various MusicGenerations programmes differ; therefore, the separate programmes produce different texts. Here we look at "Now or Never" (2012-2013) and "Talent for Freedom" (2014-2015).

"Now or Never"

A 40-minute documentary called *Now or Never* (Paul de Bont Productions) was released in 2013. It marked a period of more than 10 years during which MusicGenerations worked with talents across generations and cultural backgrounds. Analysis of this documentary allowed us to look into the previous MusicGenerations programme.

The set-up

The documentary follows the preparations for the "Now or Never" premiere. It features scenes from the premiere as well as the rehearsals. The private homes of participants and their personal preparations for the show are also shown. The plot of the 2013 show is set up to reflect an intergenerational battle. The story is that the director of a choir of seniors has passed away due to the horrible singing and lack of talent of the choir members. Consequently, the choir tries to rejuvenate by bringing in young people. However, everyone is stubborn and they have a hard time collaborating musically. The show revolves around battles between generations—in one such battle the young people sing "Young, Wild & Free" by Snoop Dogg and Wiz Khalifa, and the older people respond by singing Elvis Presley's "(You're the) Devil In Disguise"—before they finally come together in communal song.

The message

The documentary shows how the generations—the youngest participant is 14 and the oldest 87 years old—are challenged to give it their best. The message is clear: MusicGenerations' talent development is not focused on becoming famous; it is about sharing and having fun. Several scenes provide insight into the interaction between the young and the old. What becomes apparent is the mutual positive attitude—the participants all smile, laugh, and seem to enjoy one another's company. In the video, both young and old participants talk positively about the interaction between the generations and they value each other's musical contributions. The young people appreciate the life experience of the older talents, who in turn benefit from the vitality and energy of the young ones. One older female singer can be heard saying, "I feel enriched by the respect and love we receive from the younger people."

> Several scenes provide insight into the interaction between the young and the old.

Clear signs of mutual support and understanding can be identified. The documentary thus presents music as a facilitator for intergenerational communication, as a universal language uniting a diverse group of people. Ethnic and cultural diversity remain almost unarticulated throughout the documentary—suggesting that it has not explicitly been (or did not need to be) an issue or topic among the participants during the programme.

In addition to the positive effects of intergenerationality, the shared love for music regardless of one's background is centre-stage in the documentary. Music is the language through which the participants express their emotions. Their passion for music defines their personal identities. The documentary is built around personal narratives and presents viewers with the life stories of several participants and their (at times, literal) struggle for life. Here again, music is at the heart of their stories: for the participants, it is a way of living, of surviving, of not giving up. Music is what makes them happy and keeps them going. The documentary thus frames music and the ability to sing as a story of empowerment. The wife of a fragile old male singer is shown saying, "The moment he stops singing, that will be the end of him."

Hence, the three main statements of "Now or Never" concern intergenerational interaction, the unifying power of a shared passion for music, and the prospect of empowerment through music. The underlying political rationale of the programme is only briefly touched upon in the documentary, when Groot is shown explaining:

The young and the old have a lot to give each other. Society is in dire need of such interaction, both economically and socially. In that sense it is "now or never," because if we do not find ways soon to make people from all cultures and ages understand each other better and appreciate one another's contributions, at one point, it will be too late to reverse the growing alienation between the generations.

"Talent for Freedom"

The programme "Talent for Freedom," which took place from 2014 to 2015 in the cities of Groningen, Rotterdam, and Amsterdam, provides us with a second MusicGenerations text. We have been able to study the programme live.

The set-up

This programme tuned into Europe's commemoration of the end of World War II, 70 years ago, in 2015. It sets out to explore what freedom means to different ages and nationalities. MusicGenerations works with these different interpretations of (a lack of) freedom by building musical bridges among them and among the different generations, ethnicities, and cultures.

"Talent for Freedom" is advertised as a music programme with freedom as the leading theme. The programme runs the year round and participants can start at any point during this time after auditioning. The auditions are informal and people are invited to use a song of their preference. The programme follows MusicGenerations' characteristic format: a) a series of rehearsals, b) small concerts (several, starting as soon as possible), c) master classes by well-known Dutch singers or rap-stars (two or three a year), and d) a big, final concert in an established cultural venue. For instance, in 2015, small concerts were staged at the Liberation Festival Amsterdam, and in Rotterdam at North Sea around Town and Rotterdam Unlimited. This year's masters were Loulou Hameleers, Blaxtar, and YesR. The "Talent for Freedom" premieres took place in De Meervaart (the main theatre of Amsterdam Nieuw-West) and the Rotterdamse Schouwburg (the city theatre of Rotterdam).

> The auditions are informal and people are invited to use a song of their preference.

Low thresholds

The participants are amateur vocal talents, but most of them have had semi-professional experiences. Almost all of them either have been singing in the past, or are currently singing in a choir or band. Several strong (old and young) voices stand out and some of the young participants dream of a career in music. It is, however, not just the strongest voices that perform solos or in duets during concerts. Everyone indicating the wish to sing part of the lyrics of a certain song is given the opportunity. Those who shun a solo act in the spotlight simply remain part of the general choir.

Taking part in the programme and attending the concerts is free of charge.
The main message: everyone is welcome. That is one of the programme's strengths, since both the young (secondary school pupils, students) and the older participants (some of them living on a small income or pension) do not have the means to afford professional musical training. They are, however, serious in their quest for their own musical talent development. One Indonesian-Dutch older male singer, who has been with MusicGenerations ever since the Euro+ Songfestival, explains:

I greatly enjoy singing. I appreciate the fact that MusicGenerations is free of charge. I may be almost 80 years old, but that's no reason to stop improving my voice. Taking private lessons and working with professional musicians, however, is expensive. I wouldn't be able to develop myself musically if I had to take it all out of my pension.

The songs of freedom

The MusicGenerations team selects the songs to be performed during the concerts. In 2015, the selection was by theme: songs about freedom, anti-slavery, anti-discrimination, and the like. Although the MusicGenerations team selects the songs, the selection can be adjusted to the preferences and musical genres of the participants. Attention is paid so that every participant finds something to his or her liking—be it just a certain rhythm. The majority of participants indicate in the questionnaire that they feel recognised in their musical taste or cultural tradition by the team. Sometimes surprisingly so, as one girl explains, "My Kurdish heritage was already represented before I entered the group. It makes me really happy that this is the case. And above all: it is a song that I always love to sing!" The participants acknowledge that the repertoire encompasses a wide range of cultural traditions. They admit that, evidently, it could be even more inclusive of, for instance, Jewish, Turkish, or classical music traditions. But at the same time, they acknowledge that there is only so much music one can sing during one concert.

> "My Kurdish heritage was already represented before I entered the group."

The set lists of the concerts in Rotterdam and Amsterdam are composed of a wide range of musical styles (rap, pop, blues, chansons, jazz) and languages (English, Dutch, German, French, Zazaki, and Armenian). To name a few: "De gedachten zijn vrij," "Something Inside so Strong," "Where is the Love," "Lied Einer Deutschen Mutter," "Grow Old," "Redemption Song," "A Simple Song of Freedom," "None of Us are Free," "Imagine," "Fight for Your Right (to Party)," "Als de hemel valt," "Anton de Kom," "Le deserteur," "Mens durf te leven," "Kraanvogellied" (a Dutch-Armenian version of an Armenian song), and the Kurdish song "Venge Yeno." All songs are performed by a combination of people, old and young and of different ethnic backgrounds. Some songs may speak more strongly to the older participants; others seem to affect the old and young equally, e.g., "Something Inside so Strong." During the concerts, one or two songs are performed with one of the professionals who worked with the participants in the master classes. Although the participants value the opportunity to perform with a professional singer on stage, the concerts do not need these professionals to raise their profile.

The many faces of freedom

In its selection of songs, MusicGenerations shows that freedom has many faces: memories of World War II, the history of slavery, racial segregation and apartheid. Some songs refer to current civil wars and ethnic cleansing in Eastern Europe, the Balkans and the Middle East. Again, other songs allude to racism and exclusion in the Western world.

> A multitude of experiences with (losing one's) freedom is also manifest among the participants.

A multitude of experiences with (losing one's) freedom is also manifest among the participants. Young Dutch-Dutch participants from sheltered backgrounds may have never experienced oppression, may even take freedom for granted. On the other hand, an older woman was interned in a Japanese camp in Indonesia during World War II; a young girl's parents fled from Kurdistan; an older man fled from Armenia. For the Surinamese-Dutch and Antillean-Dutch participants, the history of slavery is still present. Several (young) participants interpret the concept of freedom in terms of personal freedom. Some participants experience a threat to their personal freedom due to, for instance, financial debt or deteriorating eyesight. Others refer to freedom of choice and self-definition: the freedom to be who you want to be, to construct your own identity, to love and marry whomever you want. A Turkish-Dutch girl elaborates:

For too long a time, I was a prisoner of other people's image of whom I should be or what I was supposed to do in life. Images from Turkish-Dutch people and again other images form the wider Dutch community. Freedom for me is about being able to do what I choose to do. Nowadays I can stand for what I believe in. I am an actor and love Dutch chansons and "kleinkunst" [a typically Dutch mixture of (stand-up) comedy, singing chansons and spoken word].

The message

From the account above and reading "Talent for Freedom's" stage image as text, both the concept and the message of MusicGenerations become clear. These are as simple as they are effective. First, things may not always run smoothly during the concerts, the seniors may briefly forget their lyrics, but the group—as diverse as it is in terms of age, ethnicity, and experience in stage performance—stands united on stage. The participants are one in their enjoyment of the music. Their mutual encouragement and support are clearly visible to the audience.

Second, the constantly changing stage image is loaded with strong images, ephemeral as they may be. For instance, a Turkish-Dutch girl steps back into the group after a solo and grabs hold of the hand of the Kurdish-Dutch girl standing next to her. There they are: two beautiful young women, both with beautiful voices, both struggling with their intersecting histories, but above all with finding their own place in the super-diverse context of the Netherlands. A Dutch-Dutch girl has fallen in love with the Kurdish language and sings a duet in Kurdish with the Kurdish-Dutch girl. An 80-year-old Indonesian-Dutch woman and a 16-year-old Dutch-Dutch girl hug each other in an expression of shared relief after finishing their duet of the Beatles' "Imagine." An older Dutch-Dutch woman gets so exited that she squeezes the hand of one of the young boys and they smile appreciatively at each other. A Dutch-Dutch woman, performing "Lied einer Deutschen Mutter," drives home the message to the audience that World War II also caused German citizens to suffer. Three older men of different ethnic backgrounds sing a Dutch translation of the Beastie Boys' "Fight for Your Right (to Party)," making the entire audience cheer and sing along. Goose bumps are triggered by the lyrics of the Anton de Kom-song about a Surinamese anti-colonist author and resistance fighter during World War II. Participants of different ages and colours perform the verses. The list of images could easily be extended, but the message is clear. The concert shows how different dominant narratives sound, when told through the stories of the people below, who have to carry the can for what is instigated from above (cf. Schygulla 2013, p. 131).

The gestures are spontaneous, the songs and the composition of the group are the result of a conscious choice. In this respect, the images are partly constructed. To some, they may appear as cheap imagery targeted at tear-jerking effects. Some may wonder how much truth there is in a simple image of two young girls holding hands. Others may even accuse us of shallow analysis, missing the complexity. But in our reading, such images summarise the essence of MusicGenerations' message: that very complexity is man-made; it could be this simple. The images presented by "Talent for Freedom" are not just a metaphor, they represent an everyday reality—small as it may be—and, hence, an alternative.

> The images presented by "Talent for Freedom" are not just a metaphor, they represent an everyday reality—small as it may be—and, hence, an alternative.

In Short

Comparing the texts of the two programmes, we see similarities representing the multifaceted message of the MusicGenerations programme: the different generations share a strong passion for music and singing, music can function as a bridge between generations, and the group of participants is highly diverse, but diversity is not necessarily an issue. There are also differences. The participants in "Now or Never," singing the songs of their preference, focus on individual empowerment. Moreover, "Now or Never" is more theatrical, the songs are brought together through a storyline. "Talent for Freedom" is a concert. The songs are selected using the theme of freedom; the relationship between the participants and the songs is less direct. "Talent for Freedom" is more political in its message and takes a stance against exclusion.

MusicGenerations as Social Practice — Changing Perspectives

The analysis of *social practice* contains considerations about whether the discursive practice reproduces or, instead, restructures the existing order of discourse and about what consequences this has for the broader social practice. To establish whether "Talent for Freedom" can indeed be understood as a social practice, we required insight into how the programme is experienced by its participants and audiences and how it impacted their perception and thinking. To this end, as mentioned, we held interviews with a selection of the participants and conducted a questionnaire among 39 of them. Moreover, we approached the audience with two brief questions inquiring into their experience.

By its very nature, MusicGenerations attracts people who are open-minded. It need not come as a surprise that a quarter of the participants answered that they have not come to think differently, as one of the Dutch-Dutch women illustrates when she says:

I already had good insight into the lives of people of different ages and ethnic backgrounds. Now maybe even more so, but, to me, the greatest change participating in "Talent for Freedom" has brought about is that I now know them personally.

Other participants indicate that they did indeed become (even) more open-minded as a consequence of their participation in the programme. They have come to think more positively about the other generation or their musical tastes. Almost half the participants indicate that they now perceive people from a different generation and/or different cultural backgrounds more positively, also outside the programme, when they go about their everyday lives.

Moreover, a quarter of the participants indicate in the questionnaire that they have come to realise during the programme that freedom can mean different things to different people and that, as a concept, it refers to different types of repression: the history of slavery, World War II, the Kurdish situation, personal liberation, prearranged marriages, and so on. Some of them now experience a deeper understanding of the importance and meaning of freedom. In the words of one Surinamese-Dutch older woman:

"Redemption Song" as a song never meant anything to me; I guess I have always listened superficially. But now, after I chose to sing this song, I started to pay attention to the words and they touched me. I also recite part of the Anton de Kom song. There the same thing happened. All my life, I have heard about "Anton de Kom" and "we slaves of Surinam," but only now the meaning has come across and has moved me deeply. I am being re-educated! Interesting, isn't it? I had to reach this age to be able to really hear those words.

One Dutch-Dutch girl discloses bashfully that she had hardly been aware of the history of slavery before she joined MusicGenerations (so much for the Dutch educational system!).

The songs and the concert have also driven home the message about the essentiality of diversity and freedom to the audiences. Even though the concerts are not purely professional, members of the audience are highly enthusiastic during the performances. They cheer, applaud, and sing along. The largest part of the audience is made up of family and friends of the participants. They get the message of the concert without exception, as the audience members told us when we approached them after the premieres in Rotterdam and Amsterdam. Asked for the strongest impression the concert made on them, we received answers such as:

That was seeing all ages together on stage, expressing real togetherness, jointly giving words to the importance of freedom.

The unity. The colourfulness. The liveliness. Freedom is important and we have to protect it collectively.

They all sang great, each in their own way, some in their own language, like the Armenian man. That made it really special.

Touched by the image of the Kurdish-Dutch and Turkish-Dutch girls holding hands during the performance, we sought out their families afterwards to ask them about their impressions. Their reactions underline the fact that it was not so much an empty image—"no big deal for two young girls, both raised in the Netherlands, to hold hands"—but an expression of open-mindedness on the side of the young women and their parents. When we asked the father of the Kurdish-Dutch girl about this experience, he exclaimed:

I feel honoured that our songs are being performed in places like these [the Rotterdam Schouwburg]. They sang in our language! Our language touches a sensitive spot in me. I honestly had to fight back the tears. They sang it so pure: both my daughter and the Dutch girl. It is unique that this Dutch girl has come to love and defend our language, a language that is threatened with extinction. What I realised during the concert is that in spite of all our differences, our religions and ethnic backgrounds, freedom is important to us all. Freedom is the exception, not the rule in this world. You wonder, when it can be so beautiful and in a way easy, why do we people spoil it all the time? Listening to the music here, you understand that we need one another, are dependent on one another to make peace.

While the father continues to explain the Kurdish situation, the Kurdish language and the fact that the Kurds are divided among themselves, the mother of the Turkish-Dutch girl listens to the conversation. When asked what she thinks about it, she answers, "Everybody is entitled to his own opinion. I respect that. Wasn't that exactly what this concert was all about?!"

A Moroccan-Dutch social worker was touched by the Amsterdam concert to the point where he is considering a different approach in his future work:

Young and old people singing together about freedom, that touched me deeply. Even if they think differently about the concept of freedom, they still bring the message across to the audience together. That unity: great. I got goose bumps when I became aware of certain details. For instance, one of the older women took the hand of one of the young guys. That touched me, because it revealed sincere closeness. Working with a combination of generations and with the theme of freedom is new to me. As an ambassador, I supported the programme, helped with the acquisition of participants and audiences. I will definitely think about how to integrate the intergenerational aspect in other programmes I am involved in.

In Short

The last thing we want to do is claim that one music programme is going to change the world. Nonetheless, "Talent for Freedom" can indeed be understood as a social practice in the sense that it has offered new perspectives to its participants and has made audience members think about diversity and freedom. Moreover, the text and images presented by "Talent for Freedom" present to us a reality that exists parallel to dominant narratives. In this reality, they are expressing a complexity that is more progressive than the simple stories of good or bad, right or wrong, that prevail in the dominant narratives supporting, e.g., the logic of (world) politics. As such, "Talent for Freedom's" reality can certainly be interpreted as an alternative narrative: already real, but not (yet) dominant. This is further elaborated upon in chapter 7 and 10.

How to Achieve Transformation?

This chapter's exploration of MusicGenerations as text and social practice also illustrates how one sets up a programme to successfully communicate the message of generations, diversity, and freedom. It illustrates how participants and audiences are offered an essential, positive—maybe even transformative—experience. MusicGenerations' approach can be an inspiration to others—policy makers as well as social and cultural professionals—because it combines (at least) eight elements with which it crosscuts all kinds of (policy) categories and target groups:

1. First and foremost, people are approached as talents. The MusicGenerations team values the participants for who they are and what they (dis)like. The participants' talents are taken as a starting point, not their "problems," shortcomings, diversity, or age.

2. MusicGenerations works from a super-diversity approach; from the intersection of age, ethnicity, musical tastes, etc. There is room for self-definition; the talents decide which part of their identity they will show on stage. For them it is far more pleasant to participate in a programme that gives them the opportunity to be themselves, and to be appreciated for it, than having to live up to images and identities that are ascribed to them by dominant society.

3. Rather than working only with seniors or only with young people, the team takes an intergenerational approach to age.

4. The generations, ethnicities, and cultures meet as equals; there is no hierarchy in talent, knowledge, or influence.

5. The arts are at the core of the programme, not care or welfare. It is about doing something the participants really like, about having fun. Even though music is not implemented as a means to an end, participation may well have indirect positive effects on the participants in terms of care and welfare.

6. The overall concept of the programme conveys a strong political message and a critical reflection on contemporary social practices.

7   The team positively exploits the connecting power of the shared love of music and the importance people attribute to freedom. Even if participants appreciate different musical traditions, genres or styles, they recognise themselves in one another's love for music: it is something they have in common. Hence, sharing and recognition go hand in hand with disagreement and difference in interpretation, without standing in the way of successful collaboration.

8   The team also positively exploits the power of music. This power is further explored in chapter 6.

References   Jørgensen, M. W., & Phillips, L. J. (2002). *Discourse analysis as theory and method.* London: Sage.

Schygulla, H. (2013). Wach auf und träume. München: Schirmer Mosel Literatur.

Trienekens, S., & Hillaert, W. (2015). *Art in transition: Manifesto for participatory art practices.* Brussels: Demos & Utrecht: Cal-XL.

Blaxtar and Duygu

5. Art and Dementia: Inclusive and Super-Diverse

Marjolein Gysels

Art creates opportunities to connect critically with matters of current concern, such as the ageing of the population, the increasing number of people affected by dementia, the restructuring of care systems, the exclusive channelling of funding towards technological solutions for what are basically human issues, and it interrogates the inequalities on which they are based. Such big issues are often carried by discourses that are deeply embedded in established cultural interests and are therefore left largely unquestioned. Participatory art can enhance social awareness as it requires direct involvement of those who are most closely affected and, as it addresses differences in thinking and acting which creates occasions for public and open debate. These are democratic processes in the true sense of the term, having "...a sense of—and actual engagement in—shaping society and life, particularly... in a world in which so many people are excluded from control or who experience a sense of alienation in their lives" (Lang & Rayner, 2012).

Views of Dementia

People with dementia face multiple challenges, not only inflicted by the effects of the condition itself, but also by their environment. A dementia diagnosis sets a whole set of ideas and behaviours in motion which have serious consequences for the person in question (Alzheimer's Disease International, 2012; Ballenger, 2006).

What started as "normal" forgetfulness becomes pathologised as a symptom of one of the most feared conditions of our time. In addition to the prospect of having to deal with the symptoms of a chronic illness with progressive mental impairment which will lead to increasing dependence, there are the societal prejudices that condemn the person affected to an existence considered worse than death (Gubrium, 1986). Popular understandings of dementia render it as an "emptying out of the self," thus removing what makes one human (Fontana & Smith, 1989). These malignant social constructions of dementia (Kitwood, 1997) have negative consequences for the self-esteem of those with dementia, for how they are treated by friends and family, and for their social position. Those with dementia become stigmatized and risk being subjected to oppressive caring relationships (Bond, Corner, Lilley, & Elwood., 2002). The institutional environments in which they are spending the last part of their lives generally do not offer opportunities for meaningful activities. This deprives them even further of the elements of life that feed people's interests (Chung, 2004). It exacerbates their withdrawal and leads to further deterioration in functioning.

The Voices of People with Dementia

The medical conceptualization of dementia reinforces social exclusion as it denies "cognitive citizenship" to people by limiting its understanding of dementia to mere cognitive function (Bond et al., 2002; Graham, 2004). Alternative psychological and sociological theories raise the importance of the socio-cultural context that shapes dementia, the values, beliefs, and norms that determine the response to this condition. However, these are not based on the voices of people with dementia. Existing accounts of the experiences of people with dementia come from qualitative studies, personal narratives, or from more activist individuals who are in the earlier stages of dementia and are writing to raise awareness about the condition. These accounts are typically produced by people who are in late middle age, well-educated, white, married, and professional, with strong religious or ideological beliefs and supportive families. Those who do not match this profile, are of ethnic minority backgrounds, with lower levels of education or socio-economic status remain unheard (Hulko, 2004).

In the scientific world, the need is now widely expressed for innovative methods that enable reliable and valid contributions from people with impaired cognition, to counter disempowering views of dementia and to develop alternative approaches and services that better meet the needs of those with dementia and their caregivers (Downs, 2000). But involving people with dementia in research and considering their experiences in their socio-cultural contexts is a challenging task due to the way evidence is conceptualized as a rational and unbiased representation of reality, and due to the excessive measures taken to protect those labelled as vulnerable (de Raeve, 1994; Gysels, Evans, & Higginson, 2012). Institutional care contexts and regulations form serious barriers to even approach those affected.

Art, Dementia and Super-Diversity

What people with dementia all have in common is their advanced age, and also, most are sensitive to an atmosphere that is relaxed, attentive, joyful, light, and inviting to their active presence or participation. Often people with dementia have fewer inhibitions in social interaction, which reveals complex identities connecting in multiple and unpredictable ways. These are impossible to analyse as separate elements that fall into the traditional categories of age, gender, class, race, and ethnicity. Even further removed from everyday interactions is the unifying label of dementia as it manifests with as much variation as there are personalities who live with it. These multidimensional processes, such as the ones that influence experiences of dementia in later life, are exactly what the notion of super-diversity (Vertovec, 2007) comes to grips with. It is also exactly what professional artists working with people with dementia tap into. I refer to artists who have set foot in care homes to practice their work as art (Gysels, Thwaite, & Broos, 2016) as opposed to art therapy, which is generally conducted for therapeutic purposes and falls under the remit of the medical team in care institutions.

How Art Makes a Difference

These artists practice "participatory art" and engage with the social dynamics of real life as their material, media, and inspiration (De Bruyne & Gielen, 2011). These artists most often work with groups of people; one-to-one sessions occur less frequently. They take on the role of facilitator and, depending on the stage of the illness of those involved, they may be assisted by caregivers—family, volunteers, or professional staff. Art with people with dementia is multidisciplinary as artists use drama, music, dance, visual arts, poetry, and storytelling (Basting, 2006). The artists do not necessarily work towards the production of individual works of art by the participants.

The artists usually base their interventions on their unique artistic competences and sensitivities. Through art, they enter the life worlds of people with dementia from unconventional angles. The artists tend to use methods that involve multiple senses simultaneously—as these are most successful for engaging people who are otherwise difficult to reach. They create a safe and attractive space from where they offer people with dementia materials or create an event that captures their interest. These activities offer a variety of possibilities for engaging with what is on offer, with other participants and on various levels. The activities are within their capabilities and failure-free. Moreover, people with dementia are free to respond to them in any way they choose. This can lead to surprising results, where the people with dementia get the chance to manifest themselves as lively, caring, creative, and skilful participants with rich life histories.

With creative media, these artists thus enable people with dementia to express themselves and show the entangled nature of the people's subjectivities. They also reveal other elements constitutive of identity, for example, the strategies people employ for maintaining ordinary conversations, even in the face of considerable loss of vocabulary. Artists creatively integrate such exchanges in their art sessions, while maintaining respectful mutual conversation, at the same time they transform what tends to be seen as a sign of incapacity into artistic material. This is what inspires artists, what they magnify to creatively explore, meanwhile denying commonplace ageist and disablist cultural values.

Art as a Vehicle for Inclusion

The open spaces where artists have few expectations of what is going to happen and the empathetic sharing of activities with people with dementia offer opportunities for events that reveal meaning which would go unnoticed if one stayed too focused on the usual factors that tend to be attributed to identity. Additionally, artists establish contact and communication with people with dementia. They succeed in actively involving and enthusing even those in the advanced stages of the illness, who have undergone considerable changes in their cognitive abilities. Artists are able to include a group of people in art-making who are no longer considered capable of being creative on the basis of the assumptions of a "hypercognitive" culture (Post, 1995), which has denied personhood to people with dementia and led to their marginalisation and social exclusion.

Attentive artists can thus develop insight into diverse experiences of people from different walks of life. These also include the perspectives from those groups who are missing from the research literature and other written publications. However, these subjectivities only surface under certain circumstances, and even then, there is no guarantee that they will appear. This requires longer-term artistic projects carried out by skilful artists who become acquainted with those involved and develop sensitivities to detect meaningful actions by participants. In this way, artistic projects can contribute to areas that are problematic for conventional approaches. They can fulfil important roles in decision-making regarding care and research participation. However, these art interventions need to get the space to develop, not as the short-lived subsidy-based projects they tend to be at present, but as sustained events that are integrated into mainstream care provision and community life. Then they will be able to generate results that point to different routes, question taken-for-granted practices (for example, informed consent), throw different light on principles these are based on (such as autonomy), stimulate debate, and realise social change.

References

Alzheimer's Disease International (2012). *World Alzheimer report: Overcoming the stigma of dementia.* London.

Ballenger, J. F. (2006). The biomedical deconstruction of senility and the persistent stigmatisation of old age in the United States. In A. Leibing, & L. Cohen (Eds.), *Thinking about dementia: Culture, loss, and the anthropology of senility.* New Brunswick, NJ: Rutgers University Press.

Basting, A. D. (2006). Arts in dementia care: "This is not the end... it's the end of this chapter." *Generations, 30*(1), 16-20.

Bond, J., Corner, L., Lilley, A., & Elwood, C. (2002). Medicalisation of insight and caregivers' response to risk in dementia. *Dementia, 1*(3), 313-328.

Chung, J. (2004). Activity participation and well-being of people with dementia in long term care settings. *Occupation, Participation, and Health, 24,* 22–31.

De Bruyne, P., & Gielen, P. (2011). *Community art: The politics of trespassing.* Amsterdam: Valiz.

De Raeve, L. (1994). Ethical issues in palliative care research. *Palliative Medicine, 8,* 298–305.

Downs, M. (2000). Dementia in socio-cultural context: An idea whose time has come. *Ageing and Society, 20,* 369–375.

Fontana, A,, & Smith, R. W. (1989). Alzheimer disease victims: The unbecoming of self and the normalisation of competence. *Sociological Perspectives, 32,* 35–46.

Graham, J. (2004). Cognitive citizenship: Access to hip surgery for people with dementia. *Health Care (Don Mills), 8*(3), 295–310.

Gubrium, J. (1986). *Oldtimers and Alzheimer's: The descriptive organisation of senility.* Greenwich, CT: JAI Press.

Gysels, M., Evans, C., & Higginson, I. (2012). Patient, caregiver, professional and researcher views and experiences of participating in research at the end of life: A critical interpretive synthesis of the literature. *BMC Medical Research Methodology, 12*(123).

Gysels, M., Thwaite, A., & Broos, V. (2016). *The NowHere manifesto: Art and dementia as art.* Retrieved from http://www.anthropologyinhealth.com

Hulko, W. (2004). Social science perspectives on dementia research: Intersectionality. In A. Innes, C. Archibald, & C. Murphy (Eds.), *Dementia and social inclusion: Marginalised groups and marginalised areas of dementia research, care and practice* (pp. 237–254). London: Jessica Kingsley.

Kitwood, T. (1997). *Dementia reconsidered: The person comes first.* Buckingham: Open University Press.

Lang, T., & Rayner, G. (2012). Ecological public health: The 21st century's big idea? An essay by Tim Lang and Geof Rayner. *BMJ, 345,* e5466. doi: 10.1136/bmj.e5466

Post, S. (1995). *The moral challenge of Alzheimer's disease.* Baltimore: Johns Hopkins Press.

Vertovec, S. (2007). Super-diversity and its implications. *Ethnic and Racial Studies, 30*(6), 1024–1054.

Astrid & Lisa

6. Music: Playful Power for the Personal and the Political

Eltje Bos

> "On one thing most scholars of the impact of music agree: music is an incredibly powerful (emotional) force..."

On one thing most scholars of the impact of music agree: music is an incredibly powerful (emotional) force (Garofalo, 2010). However, its force can be used to achieve highly disparate goals. For instance, music's capacity to generate positive feelings and emotions, is used in the public domain to influence activities such as buying behaviour or to force people into a calm mood in public spaces. Garofalo (2010) describes how music can be exclusionary. Music organizes society into sub groups or subcultures. Music can be used to promote patriotism and national identity, distinguishing the in-group from the out-group. In national contexts, for instance, music is used to mobilize citizens by singing a national anthem. At public events, such as a soccer match, songs distinguish the supporters of one team from the others. In authoritarian regimes, music is employed as part of the propaganda machine. In the past, music, visual arts, theatre, and film have been used by various oppressive regimes to propagate their ideological view: the former Soviet Union, North Korea, and Nazi Germany are a few examples. At the other end of the spectrum, we find examples in which music's capacity to mobilize people is used as a force for resistance and/or solidarity. Music—protest songs—play a distinct role in the resistance against repression.

> "Solidarity is often the goal when music is used..."

Solidarity is often the goal when music is used as a means to build bridges and unite people or to help people in need as was the case, e.g., with Band Aid and Live Aid (Garofalo, 2010). As we will come to see, making music and singing tends to generate a feeling of togetherness and triggers our emotions—but it does so whatever the aims of the gathering. This means that, if art is to work for solidarity or as a device to create tolerance, it should be directed at doing so.

This chapter explores how and in what context participation in the arts contributes to positive feelings, which result in enhanced individual and group skills and empowerment, which in turn, will positively benefit society and the creation of public value. This is an urgent matter for several reasons. The cultural and social dynamics in western welfare states, such as the Netherlands, demand changes on many levels. The roles of citizens are changing as a consequence of the aging population, the financial and economic crisis, huge cutbacks in governmental spending, and governmental decentralization processes. Moreover, the current arrival of large numbers of refugees, and the subsequent tensions between groups of people, combined with the rise of a network society, cry for creative solutions to create public value for *all* citizens. Elsewhere in this volume, Trienekens argues that citizenship in a post-multicultural context demands skills that enable all citizens, with their various backgrounds and needs, to participate in a shared public democratic culture consisting of relationships built around shared interests and needs. These skills are also known as transversal skills: the skill to listen, to debate, to be empathic, and to resolve conflicts. Nussbaum (2013) describes the values of a "just" society, in which people of all ages, cultural and social backgrounds can participate in an environment of equality, inclusion, and distribution. An advisory committee to the Dutch Ministry of Culture and Education writes that "in our future education the emphasis is on participating in a democratic society and about respect for each other" (Onsonderwijs2032.nl).

Practices in the field of community development show that these skills, and other competencies needed in contemporary society, do not come automatically, but must be cultivated by citizens, civil servants, policy makers, and professionals in a wide variety of domains. It calls for different forms of interaction. Music Generations, however small its programmes may be, can be understood as a practical example and forerunner of these new forms of interaction. In this chapter, I set out to explore how it is that participation in the arts can have a positive societal impact (cf. Bos, 2015). To make a case for the arts, I venture into various academic disciplines. First, I explore how positive feelings are generated, according to psychologists, and with the help of insights from sociology, I explore the benefits for groups and the broader society. In the second part, I focus on the arts, especially on music. How does it generate emotions, what emotions are evoked, and in what context will participation in the arts benefit or contribute to the skills needed in a democratic "just" society?

Positive Emotions, Emotional Energy, and Play

The end of the last century saw increased interest in positive psychology. The work of scholars such as Csikszentmihalyi (1997) and Frederickson (1998) intended to counter the dominant focus on negative emotions in psychology. These emotions tend to narrow people's thinking as well as their focus, and are the cause of many problems for people and their environment. Negative emotions also tend to narrow people's "thought-action repertoire." Positive psychology looks at positive emotions and their impact on an individual.

In his theory, Csikszentmihalyi (1990; 1997) outlines that people are happiest when they experience a state of "flow." He even maintains that possessions and income above an elementary level of living are not contributing to happiness, but the—repeated—experience of flow does. This is a state of concentration or complete absorption with the activity at hand and the situation. In an interview with *Wired* magazine, Csikszentmihalyi described flow as "being completely involved in an activity for its own sake. This is a feeling everyone has at times, characterized by a feeling of great absorption, engagement, fulfilment, and skill" (Geirland, 1996). The ego falls away. Time flies. One forgets to eat. Every action, movement, and thought follows the previous one almost automatically. One's whole being is involved and skills are used optimally. To reach a state of flow, people need a goal and the skills to reach it. All kinds of activities can lead to this state, e.g., ironing, repairing motorbikes, singing, and dancing.

In 1998, Frederickson published an article called *What good are positive emotions?* The purpose of the article is "to introduce a new model of the form and function of a subset of discrete positive emotions." Not only does she aim to level the uneven knowledge base between negative and positive emotions; she also intends to enhance "applications and interventions that might improve individual and collective functioning, psychological well-being, and physical health" (Frederickson, 1998). She refers to a wide range of research literature, including her own, to show how—repeated—positive emotions influence people's thinking and acting (thought-action repertoire). People who experience repeated positive emotions feel better, and are more open. This, in turn, has the effect of building the individual's physical, intellectual, and social resources. Frederickson refers to this finding as the "Broaden and Built" model. This model thus assumes that positive emotions are necessary for sound individual and collective functioning. Frederickson more specifically describes the form and function of a subset of positive emotions: including joy, interest, contentment, and love. She considers these emotions to be fundamental human resources with multiple advances. Positive emotions build and broaden the thought- action repertoire, and counter lingering negative emotions. They also fuel psychological resilience, and help to develop this resilience; thus they contribute to an upward spiral to enhanced emotional wellbeing. These positive emotions she refers to can be evoked by a wide variety of activities, and among those the active and receptive participation in arts (and culture).

> "to introduce a new model of the form and function of a subset of discrete positive emotions."

Joy

As Frederickson (1998) explores the emotions of joy, interest, contentment, and love, she looks at their conceptual space, how the thought-action repertoire is constructed, and what its possible effects are. Joy, she writes, shares conceptual space with other relatively high-arousal positive emotions such as amusement, elation, and gladness (cf. de Rivera et al., 1989). Joy is often used interchangeably with happiness (Lazarus, 1986) and feelings of joy arise in contexts appraised as safe and familiar. She quotes Frijda (1986) to underpin the action tendency associated with joy. Frijda refers to it as free activation: "[it] is in part aimless, unasked-for readiness to engage in whatever interaction presents itself and in part readiness to engage in enjoyments" (in Frederickson, 1998, p. 304).

According to Frederickson, joy creates the urge to play and to be playful in the broadest sense of the word, encompassing not only physical and social play, but also intellectual and artistic play. The urge to play represents a generic, nonspecific thought-action tendency. Joy and related positive emotions can thus be described as broadening an individual's thought-action repertoire. Joy can have the incidental effect of building an individual's physical, intellectual, and social skills. These new resources, she argues, are long-lasting and can be drawn from, long after the instigating experience of joy has subsided.

Interest

Interest is, in Frederickson's view, sometimes used interchangeably with curiosity, intrigue, excitement, or wonder, and shares conceptual space with challenge and intrinsic motivation (Deci & Ryan, 1985). Interest arises in contexts appraised as safe and as offering novelty, change, and a sense of possibility (Izard, 1977) or mystery (Kaplan, 1992). The momentary thought-action tendency sparked by interest, according to Izard (1977), is exploration, explicitly and actively aimed at increasing knowledge of and experience with the target of interest. Importantly, the openness to new ideas, experiences, and actions is what characterises the mind-set of interest as broadened, rather than narrower.

Interest also builds the individual's store of knowledge. Again, this store of knowledge becomes a long-lasting resource that can be accessed in later moments. DeNora (2010) shows how Izard (1977) pushed this idea further, for he understands interest as the primary instigator of personal growth, creative endeavour, and the development of intelligence.

Contentment

Contentment is, in Frederickson's view (1998), often used interchangeably with other low-arousal positive-emotion terms such as tranquillity or serenity, and shares conceptual space with mild or receptive joy (Izard, 1977). As she explores various theoretical writings on contentment and related positive emotions, she suggests (referring to De Rivera et al., 1989; Izard, 1977), that "this emotion prompts individuals to savour their current life circumstances and recent successes, experience "oneness" with the world around them, and integrate recent events and achievements into their overall self-concept and world view." She links contentment to the work of Csikszentmihalyi (1990) by describing it to be the positive emotion that follows the stage of flow. Associations with integration, receptiveness, and increasing self-complexity characterise contentment as an emotion that broadens individuals' momentary thought-action repertoires and builds their personal resources.

Love

Love theorists acknowledge that love is not a single emotion and that people experience varieties of love, e.g., romantic or passionate love, compassionate love, caregiver love, or the attachment to caregivers. Frederickson holds the position that love experiences are made up of many positive emotions, including interest, joy, and contentment. She refers to Izard, who maintains that "acquaintances or friends renew your interest by revealing new aspects of themselves and the resulting increase in familiarity (deeper knowledge of the person) brings joy (and contentment)" (in Frederickson, 1998, p. 308). Frederickson points out that this cycle is repeated endlessly in lasting friendships or love relationships. And this helps to "build and solidify an individual's social resources" (Frederickson, 1998, p. 308). These social resources, like intellectual and physical resources, can be accumulated and drawn from at later times.

> "acquaintances or friends renew your interest by revealing new aspects of themselves and the resulting increase in familiarity (deeper knowledge of the person) brings joy (and contentment)"

Rituals

The findings of the sociologist Collins (2004), in spite of his different disciplinary approach, are more or less similar. Repeated positive experiences do generate a more positive view of people about themselves and people tend to become more closely connected with the people with whom they share this experience. This effect is not, as Frederickson sees it, a casual effect of such an experience. In Collins' reasoning, these feelings are generated through the collective experience of rituals. Collins sees a ritual as a ceremony, the going through a set of stereotyped actions where emotions are shared. A ritual is an amplifier of emotion; we as people are literally stimulated or even aroused by a successful ritual. Such a ritual can be a sports event, a great lecture, sex, or a cultural event. During a ritual, emotional charge is built up from entrainment: the micro coordination between participants' gestures, eye contact, and other forms of physical resonance with others involved, thus emotions are shared.

To be with other people during a concert generates a different energy than the one we perceive when listening to a concert alone at home. Especially when the public participates in one way or the other. Collins argues that repeated positive ritual experiences generate emotional energy. This energy makes them think more positively about themselves and the people in their group, and from there, a feeling of solidarity rises among the group members. Moreover, they carry this emotional energy with them, also outside the context of the ritual. Referring to Frederickson, joy and interest might play an important role in these rituals. Similarly, Sennett points to and elaborates on the pleasures of working together in *The Rituals, Pleasures, and Politics of Cooperation* (2012).

Play

Much earlier, in the 1930s, the Dutch historian Huizinga (1938) wrote in his book *Homo Ludens* about the role of play for people and its impact on society. He points out how play, and he includes concerts, theatre, film, and sports in his concept of play, is enacted outside reason, duty, and truth. Agreements about a time slot, the rules, and the place where it is enacted distinguishes play from the real; it is a free space next to and outside of the real. Huizinga even noted that people participating as a group in a play activity are connected, just because they do something special or even secret, not shared by others in the real world. The actual difference between "playing" in a cultural activity and playing in an activity such as sports is that it calls on creativity. The participants create something (new). There are some rules, and within those, a lot of freedom. In sports as a play, the creative space is more limited. Play in sports generally has a competitive character and a relatively tight set of rules apply.

> The actual difference between "playing" in a cultural activity and playing in an activity such as sports is that it calls on creativity.

In short

Both Collins and Huizinga thus maintain that positive experiences evoke positive emotions. These emotions help people to think more positively about themselves and help them to raise their self-esteem. People with a positive view of themselves tend to have a more open attitude toward the people around them. According to Collins, the collective experience of a ritual generates emotional energy, which, once it is evoked in people, is maintained. This emotional energy also functions outside the circle where it was generated. Frederickson then shows that people, due to their—repeated—emotions of joy, interest, contentment and love, are more open to and interested in the broader environment. Their attitude is more open and receptive due to their positive experiences, personal growth, and a sense of control over one's life that comes with it. She does not explicitly address the impact of emotions generated by group activities, as Huizinga and Collins do. But she too finds that, when people participated in a group and experienced the pleasure of working together, they tended to become more interested in their group members, in people outside their group, and more willing to do something for them. These positive experiences can be generated through various activities, including the arts. The arts can be considered to be particularly interesting, as they seem to foster the exploration of creativity, of new ways of thinking and acting.

Researching Music (Arts) and Emotion

Although few would disagree with the assertion that to participate in arts and culture is beneficial for the people involved, it is not yet fully understood *how* positive emotions can be evoked through participation in arts and culture and how the impact of the arts on individuals, their social environment, and society at large, comes about. However, more and more research becomes available showing that people experience positive feelings or emotions when participating in the arts (Matarasso, 1997; McCarthy, Ondaatje, Zakaras, & Brooks, 2004; Trienekens & van Miltenberg, 2009; Van den Hoogen, Elkhuizen, & van Maanen, 2010; Belfiore, 2010; LKCA, 2013; Scherder, 2015). Especially, the effect of music has been researched by various academic disciplines. "Music and emotion," for instance, is the subject of an impressive handbook by Juslin and Soboda (2010). It illustrates how music has been used in a number of applications in society that presume its effectiveness in evoking emotions: marketing, film, and music therapy. It too shows the positive effect music can have on individuals in various contexts.

Research into the impact of music is conducted in a wide range of academic disciplines. The brief exploration of several of these disciplines allows us to accumulate insight into the workings of music and/or art in general.

Neurobiology

Among others, Scherder (2015), Koelsch, Siebel, & Fritz (2010), Peretz (2010), and Sacks (2010) researched, from the perspective of neurobiology, what happens in our brains when we listen to or make music. Scherder (2015), for instance, describes how art challenges our brain and causes excitement, feelings of love for what we see, listen to, or experience. This is caused by the interplay of the brainstem, the amygdala and the prefrontal cortex. The brain is stimulated by listening to music, looking at visual art, and even more so by actively playing music or creating art. The reward circuit is activated and one longs for more. For our understanding of music's impact on emotions, it is important to know that, when we participate in the arts, primal parts of our brains are also triggered. This corresponds to different parts of the brain than the cognitive ones; the primal parts are beyond our direct control.

In a project called "Strong Experiences with Music" (Gabrielson, 2006, 2010), over five hundred people were asked to describe their strongest, most intense experience of music that they have ever had. The reactions people described were classified in a variety of categories. Among the experiences people described were physiological reactions such as tears and thrills, goose bumps, muscle tension, and perspiration. Behavioural actions were also registered such as jumping and clapping, moments of complete absorption, and loss of control. Respondents even mentioned existential and transcendental experiences.

Hodges (2010), based on his meta-analysis of more than fifty studies on psycho-physiological effects of music, classifies the effects in various categories such as skin conductance, heart or pulse rate, respiration, blood pressure, muscular tension, temperature, gastric motility, and various other phenomena. Among his many findings, he states that stimulating, arousing music tends to cause an increase in heart rate, while sedative music tends to cause the opposite. Some of the studies find a similar connection for blood pressure, but other studies do not. Hodges confirms the idea of people experiencing chills, thrills; such as shivering, goose bumps, tingling along the spine, and he explores how listeners respond to music with body movements, i.e., physiologically. Most studies in his meta-analysis underpin the idea that music, in various ways, stimulates the uncontrollable primal parts of our brain, next to other brain parts that we can influence (more or less).

This finding helps us to understand why music has such an impact: it (also) has an effect on the areas of our brain that we either cannot (brainstem) or only partly (limbic system) influence, which makes listening or playing music, in a sense, a "magical," powerful experience.

Social Psychology

From the perspective of social psychology, Juslin and Västfäll (2008) consider emotion to be a construct, which points to a set of phenomena of feelings, bodily behaviours, and bodily reactions that occur together in everyday life. The task of emotion psychology is to describe these phenomena and to explain them in terms of their underlying processes. The explanations can be formulated at different levels: feelings, types of information processing, and on a hardware level (brains, hormones, genes). They state that the emotional response to music occurs in a complex interaction between the music, the listener, and the context. As such, extra-musical variables influence emotional responses. For instance, goals and motives of listeners play an important role (see also DeNora 2010). Psychologists agree that emotions are biologically based, but also acknowledge a range of socio-cultural influences.

Like some of the neurobiologists, psychologists also find that music not only transfers emotions, but also evokes them. Moreover, Juslin & Västfäll's (2008) findings show that music evokes mainly positive emotions in listeners. They point out the most frequently reported responses by their respondents to music were "calm contentment" and "happiness elation" (more than 50 per cent of the emotions reported), while negative emotions such as anger-irritation or anxiety-fear only occurred in five per cent of the cases. According to Juslin and Västfäll, positive emotions were also more prevalent in musical than in non-musical events. Additionally, they found an emotional change during the musical episode and almost ninety per cent of the changes were positive. Juslin and Sloboda (2010) maintain that musical emotions are evoked through the activation of one or more mechanisms, each incorporating a distinct type of information processing. Juslin and Västfall (2008) described these mechanisms as brain stem reflexes, emotional contagion, visual imagery, episodic memory, and musical expectancy.

These findings help us understand that music not only transfers, but also evokes emotions. The brainstem reflexes are mentioned both by neurobiologists and psychologists. The psychological studies added insight into complementary mechanisms such as emotional contagion, episodic memory, and musical expectancy are added. What emotions are evoked in a particular person depends on the goals, motives, and context of the listener or performer. It is also important to note that music mainly evokes positive emotions. These findings deepen our understanding of how music is a powerful force.

Sociology of Music

The music sociologist DeNora (2010) shows us some important findings of research on music and sociology. She maintains that Collins' work on rituals and emotional energy, (re)created space for emotions in the domain of sociology. She explores how people appropriate music as a resource for emotional experience. People link forms of music to forms of social life as part of their on-going constitution of their life worlds and themselves (cf. Hall, 1986). People use music as a resource to construct their identity and to create and maintain a variety of feelings. DeNora refers to this as "aesthetic agency"; she uses this term "to highlight the consumption of aesthetic media as a means for self-interpretation and self-constitution" (2010, p. 168). She shows, by referring to studies by Gomart (1999) and herself (DeNora, 2000, 2010), how music is used as a device for "emotional work": "the bodily cooperation with an image, a thought, a memory; a cooperation of which the individual is aware" (1999, p. 171). In these studies respondents describe how they use music "to regulate moods and energy levels, to maintain desired states of feeling (e.g. relaxation, excitement) or to diminish or modify undesirable emotional states (e.g. stress, fatigue)" (DeNora, 2010, p. 171). Other studies show (Batt Rawden, 2006) that people with chronic diseases can learn to use music to regulate their emotions in order to manage and cope with their situation. In a contribution by Thaut (2010) on active and passive methods of music therapy, this is confirmed. Active methods involve making (playing) music, and receptive ones listening to music.

Social and Political Sciences

DeNora (2010, p. 163) quotes Martin (1995) on the idea of how music can be an important means for social action. Martin describes music as the non-cognitive basis of the ability and the will to act and to engage in social action. Music helps people to feel and become conscious of a situation. Matarasso (1997), for instance, found that arts projects can nurture local democracy. Participation in (community) arts encourages people to become more active citizens and strengthens their support for local and self-help projects. In one of his studies, after participating in an art project, almost two-thirds of the participants indicated that they were willing to participate in other community projects (Matarasso, 1997).

Obviously, there is also the notion of music as protest, as resistance against repressive regimes as the introduction to this article mentioned. Music can be interpreted as providing political guidance. As was already described by Eyermen and Jamieson in an interview with a participant looking back at how they treated Bob Dylan's music during his period in Students for Democratic Society in the 1960's: "We followed his career as if he was singing our songs: we got in the habit of asking where he was taking us next" (1998, p. 116). In this respect, music plays a role in the structure of social collective action. It works as a prescriptive device of agency (in its dynamics, sounds, harmonies, and textures) through which people can appreciate themselves as agents with particular capacities for social action.

Another illustration of the socio-political impact of music is its contribution to conflict resolution. Music can function as a means for transforming existing emotional dynamics between adverse groups. Chapter 2 referred to Syrious Mission's work in Syrian refugee camps in Lebanon and the West-Eastern Divan Orchestra of Arab and Israeli musicians. The idea of resolving conflicts through music may possibly be too ambitious. Still, people of conflicting groups meet one another in music or arts activities and get to know one another. Sharing their passion for singing and playing music (or theatre, for that matter) can contribute to mutual understanding. Bergh (2007, in DeNora, 2010, p. 177) points out that it seemed important to avoid wishful thinking or the over-estimation of music's great capacities. Nonetheless, we should remain open to the actual findings showing that "despite its reputation as a 'universal language,' music's powers operate (...) typically via grassroots appropriations of music, which themselves require unpacking if music is to become an effective resource for the resolution of conflicts."

The question of *how* such impact comes about is not addressed in studies such as the ones mentioned here. With the help of the research on positive psychology, their findings can however be better understood and interpreted as a result of the positive emotions (joy, interest, contentment, and love) people experience during arts projects, and the effect these emotions have on their thought-action repertoire.

Impact on the Personal, the Social and Society

Maton (2008), in his empowerment theory, perceives of a setting where making and listening to music are shared, as an empowering setting. Such settings are distinctive as they contribute at the same time to psychological, social, and civic empowerment (Maton & Brodsky, 2011).

On a personal, psychological level, we know music and other art forms can generate positive experiences, as they evoke positive emotions. We know music is a powerful force and this seems also to be likely for other art forms. Art, and especially music, is highly forceful since it triggers primordial layers of our brain, next to more cognitive layers. Having repeated positive experiences helps people to feel better, to develop (more) self-esteem, to be of value, and be worthy and to "allow themselves to be," and thus to open up their thought-action repertoire.

When it comes to the experience and connection on a social group level, music seems to be a powerful means for (amateur) musicians and the public to engage in a "ritual," and by doing so, develop an interest in, and respect and appreciation for, and a connection with people of various backgrounds, beliefs, and ideas. Moreover, research showed that people who feel positive and develop emotional energy also become more interested in others outside the group with which they were involved in positive experiences. Also, they seem to be more willing to do something for others who are not so fortunate. This new openness, through (repeated) positive experiences, especially when they are experienced as a group, also contribute to people's ability to listen, to be empathic, and thus to resolve conflicts.

> Moreover, research showed that people who feel positive and develop emotional energy also become more interested in others outside the group with which they were involved in positive experiences.

The consequences of cultural participation—such as making music and singing—for personal empowerment and the functioning in and of groups are important prerequisites in a well-functioning, inclusive, and democratic post-multicultural society.

MusicGenerations' "Talent for Freedom"

The majority of studies on the impact of music focus on passive consumption of music, i.e., listening to music. There are, however, sound reasons to think that active participation will have an even stronger impact. MusicGenerations allows for active participation. However small, MusicGenerations could function as an example for future—educational—approaches.

MusicGenerations is a unique meeting place where people come together to sing; people from various backgrounds and age groups. As they get together to sing, they collectively engage in a playful ritual. Enjoying the pleasure of singing together, the older and younger people from various backgrounds connect in a friendly, non-hierarchical way and they become interested in one another. Talents with Kurdish-Dutch, Turkish-Dutch, Dutch-Dutch, Surinamese-Dutch and other backgrounds share the stage. An 80-year-old talent sings a duet with a 16-year-old, as equals. Through the shared experience of singing, they get to know and appreciate one another. This is obviously an outcome of the context created by the MusicGenerations organisation, paired with the power of music to speak to the non- or partly-controllable parts of the brain. This helps people to forget all kinds possible hesitations of a more cognitive nature and lets them just enjoy the skills and the presence of other people.

Music triggers mainly positive emotions and people tend to open up when they experience repeated positive emotions. The joy of singing together generates an interest in the other and in what they carry with them as singers. It so happens that the "Talent for Freedom" participants sing songs they weren't interested in before. For instance, a Indonesian-Dutch lady who shifted her musical interest away from romantic songs to songs with rather more politically charged lyrics and a Dutch-Dutch girl started loving the Kurdish language and music during the programme. She had never heard a Kurdish song before.

The "Talent for Freedom" programme also showed that singing together, and the joy and togetherness it generates, seems to be stronger than the urge to emphasise the different (ideologically- or historically-based) emotions evoked by songs of freedom. Working with a diverse set list—with songs referencing various contexts of freedom—helped in this particular context—the positive experience of singing together—to create more awareness about the meaning freedom has to the individual participants. Indeed, the songs had different meanings for the various people, depending on their context, age, and experience. For one, it triggers thoughts of the history of slavery, whereas others refer to struggles for personal freedom. In the programme, these differences in evoked emotions exist, but are unproblematic.

Through the pleasure of making music together, the positive emotions this evokes, even more so when it is repeated, people develop self-esteem and interest in one another. Research shows that the effect of these experiences even carry further, beyond the group, in their thought-action repertoire, and people's increased willingness to do something for others, such as their community. This is an important step toward participation in a shared public democratic culture of a "just" society.

References

Belfiore, E., & Bennett, O. (2010). *The social impact of the arts*. New York: Palgrave McMillan.

Bergh, A. (2007). I'd like the world to sing: Music and conflict transformation. *Musicae Scientiae, Special Issue 2007 (Music Matters)*, 141–157.

Bos, E. (2015). *Twee oren en één mond*. Inaugural speech. Amsterdam: Amsterdam University of Applied Sciences.

Collins, R. (2004). *Interaction Ritual Chains*. Princeton, NJ: Princeton University Press.

Csikszentmihalyi, M. (1990). *Flow: The psychology of engagement with everyday life*. New York: HarperCollins.

Csikszentmihalyi, M. (1997). *Finding flow: The psychology of engagement with everyday life*. New York: Basic Books.

DeNora, T. (2010). Emotion as social emergence: Perspectives from music sociology. In P, N, Juslin, & J. A. Sloboda (Eds.), *Handbook of music and emotion* (pp. 159–183). Oxford: Oxford University Press.

Fredrickson, B. L. (1998). What good are positive emotions? *Review of General Psychology, 2*, 300–319.

Fredrickson, B. L., Cohn, M. A., Coffey, K. A., Pek, J., & Finkel, S. M. (2008). Open hearts build lives: Positive emotions, induced through loving-kindness meditation, build consequential personal resources. *Journal of Personality and Social Psychology, 95*, 1045–1062.

Gabrielson, A. (2006) Strong experiences elicited by music—What Music? In P. Locher, C. Martindale, & L. Dorfman (Eds), *New directions in aesthetica, creativity and the psychology of art*. Amityville, NY : Baywood.

Gabrielson, A. (2010). Strong experiences with music. In P. N. Juslin, & J. A. Sloboda (Eds.), *Handbook of music and emotion*. Oxford: Oxford University Press.

Garofalo, R. (2010). Politics, mediation, social context, and public use. In P. N. Juslin, & J. A. Sloboda (Eds.), *Handbook of music and emotion* (pp. 725–754). Oxford: Oxford University Press.

Geirland, J. (1996). Go with the Flow. *Wired*, Issue 4.09.

Hoogen, Q. van den, Elkhuizen, S., & Maanen, H. van (2010). Kringen in de vijver – Hoe meetbaar zijn maatschappelijke effecten van cultuurparticipatiebeleid? *Jaarboek Cultuurparticipatie*.

Hodges, D. A. (2010). Psychophysiological measures. In P. N. Juslin, & J. A. Sloboda (Eds.), *Handbook of music and emotion* (pp. 279–312). Oxford: Oxford University Press.

Huizinga, J. (1938, 2010). *Homo Ludens*. Amsterdam: Amsterdam University Press.

Juslin, P. N., & Sloboda, J. A. (Eds.). (2010). *Handbook of music and emotion*. Oxford: Oxford University Press.

Juslin, P. N., & Västfäll, D. (2008). Emotional responses to music: The need to consider underlying mechanisms. *Behavioral and Brain Sciences, 31*, 559–575.

Koelsch, S., Siebel, W. A., & Fritz, T. (2010). Functional neuroimaging. In P. N. Juslin, & J.A. Sloboda (Eds.), *Handbook of music and emotion* (pp. 313–346). Oxford: Oxford University Press.

Maton, K. I. (2008). Empowering community settings: Agents of individual development, community betterment, and positive social change. *American Journal of Community Psychology, 41*(1-2), 4–21.

Maton, K. I., & Brodsky, A. E. (2011). Empowering community settings: Theory, research and action. In M. Aber, K. I. Maton, & E. Seidman (Eds.), *Empowering settings and voices for social change*. Oxford: Oxford University Press.

Matarasso, F. (1997). *Use or ornament: The social impact of participation in the arts*. London: Comedia.

McCarthy, K. F., Ondaatje, E. H., Zakaras, L., & Brooks, L. (2004). *Gifts of the muse: Reframing the debate about the benefits of the arts*. Santa Monica, CA: Rand.

Nussbaum, M. C. (2013). *Political emotions*. Cambridge, MA: The Belknap Press of Harvard University Press.

Onsonderwijs2032.nl (2016) – website consulted at http://onsonderwijs2032.nl/

Peretz, I. (2010). Towards a neurobiology of musical emotions. In P. N. Juslin, & J.A. Sloboda (Eds.), *Handbook of music and emotion* (pp. 99–126), Oxford: Oxford University Press.

Scherder, E. (2015). Actieve en passieve kunstbeoefening goed voor de hersenen. *Boekman, 104*, 4–8.

Seligman, M. E. P., & Csikszentmihalyi, M. (2000). Positive psychology: An introduction. *American Psychologist, 55*, 5–14.

Sennett, R. (2012). *Together: The rituals, pleasures, and politics of cooperation*. New Haven: Yale University Press.

Thaut, M. H., & Wheeler, B. L. (2010). Music Therapy. In P. N. Juslin, & J. A. Sloboda (Eds.), *Handbook of music and emotion* (pp. 819–848). Oxford: Oxford University Press.

Trienekens, S. & Miltenburg. L. van (2009). *De Zingende Stad: Sociale en culturele effecten van een kunstproject*. Amsterdam: Hogeschool van Amsterdam.

Paul Mayer

PART II

TOWARDS POST-MULTICULTURAL CITIZENSHIP

7. 15 Years of MusicGenerations

Its Dialectical Relationship with Cultural and Integration Policy

Sandra Trienekens

This chapter explores 15 years of MusicGenerations' musical programmes, from "Euro+ Songfestival" in 2001 to "Talent for Freedom" in 2015. The developments are described against the backdrop of developments with regard to diversity and age in national and local cultural policy and integration policy discourses. As such, in the terminology of critical discourse analysis (see chapter 4), it describes the discursive practice of MusicGenerations. The analysis of discursive practice generally focuses on how authors of texts draw on already existing discourses and genres to create a text, and on how receivers of texts also apply available discourses and genres in the consumption and interpretation of the texts. This chapter's explorations reveal the interesting dialectical nature of the development of MusicGenerations' music programmes and discourse on diversity, age, or intergenerationality in policies on integration and in cultural diversity in the arts.

The information for this chapter was obtained from several interviews with Conny Groot, founder of the Euro+Songfestival Foundation, and supplemented by an analysis of documentation on MusicGenerations and a brief policy and literature review. This chapter shows that MusicGenerations' approach was *avant-garde* every step of the way. The aim is not to present an exhaustive account, but to show how the political and public debate on diversity and integration became ever more exclusionary, while MusicGenerations continued to formulate ever more complex notions of diversity and the role of ethnicity in people's identities. This happened partly in response to developments in society, and partly as a result of everyday experiences in working with the participants in the MusicGenerations programmes. The dialectical relationship is thus of a rather contrasting nature.

> This chapter shows that MusicGenerations' approach was avant-garde every step of the way.

Simultaneously, it thus becomes apparent that MusicGenerations—in spite of the long-term and continuous nature of its programmes—has not been able to change the dominant discourse on diversity and age in the realm of policy making and funding for the arts. Super-diversity (intersectionality) and intergenerationality as guiding concepts have not reached the heart of policy yet. That requires a *movement* of practices and voices; a single cultural initiative will never suffice.

The Early Years

In 2001, the year in which the Dutch city of Rotterdam was Cultural Capital of Europe, Groot started working with senior talents, specifically first generation migrant seniors, in the programme "Euro+ Songfestival." With this programme, she intended to make the overall Cultural Capital programme more representative of Rotterdam's population. City statistics indicated 160 different countries of origin for Rotterdam's citizens in 2001 (COS, 2011), but this ethnic and cultural diversity was not visible on the city's cultural stages. Groot also noticed that, at the time, Dutch research on participation in the arts hardly paid attention to migrant seniors. If they were mentioned at all, it was this generation's lack of cultural participation in mainstream, publicly funded arts that was pointed out. With the "Euro+ Songfestival," Groot set out to show that, with the "right approach," migrant seniors would participate just as easily as other citizens and that "culturally diverse art" could be just as interesting to a wider audience as any other artistic expression.

Groot's intentions proved to be quite a mission, because the Dutch cultural sector found itself, at the time, in a huge debate over the question of diversity in the arts. Around the turn of the century, several policy papers had been launched that, for the first time, seriously aimed at mainstreaming "culturally diverse art." Many established cultural organisations were far from pleased. Up until then, as Bos (2012) shows, cultural policy had focused on the cultural expressions of migrants, organised in specific programmes closely related to welfare policies and with tiny budgets; it had left the established arts and cultural organisations largely untouched.

In the meantime, evidence began to pile up that both young people and people with a background of migration preferred, and indeed participated, in other forms of culture than those funded by the government (Rijpma et al., 2000; OC&W, 2002, p. 242; RvC, 2002). This was to be corrected by cultural policy, and for a while, the national government took a positive approach to cultural diversity in the arts. The Ministry for Culture launched the national "Action Plan Cultural Diversity" (OC&W, 1999a) and interpreted confrontation and multiculturalism as enrichment for society. It optimistically called its 2001-2004 national cultural policy paper "Culture as

Confrontation" (OC&W, 1999b). Also, the Rotterdam city council invested in what it called "minority-ethnic culture" from a positive perspective built on the assumption that creating space for cultural expressions of migrant groups would strengthen their bond with the city (see Trienekens, 2004, p. 134). Groot's programme thus signified an actual practice of this new development in cultural policy to which the larger and established cultural institutions responded far less rapidly.

Building a Positive, Inclusive Approach

Even though the "Euro+ Songfestival" essentially "showcased" the ethnic cultural traditions of the migrant seniors in 2001, the approach also held a key to involving migrant seniors in the arts. Groot's method was quite simple: she visited all parts of town inviting seniors to participate and collaborate with students of Codarts, the Rotterdam music academy. Groot: "The 'right' approach was nothing more than asking the migrant seniors what the music of their heart, their heritage, was." The seniors loved the attention, and even more, liked being approached as *talented* people who had brought their cultural capital to the Netherlands. Before Groot knew, the small concerts she organised around town were a success and she proceeded to invite the participants to join the Grand Finale in De Doelen, Rotterdam's main concert hall. This concert proved to be an even bigger success, attracting an audience of 2000 people. Audience research (Richards et al., 2002) found that the majority of them hardly ever visited publicly funded art, but were now willing to give it a chance.

Looking back at these early years, Groot attributes the success of her programme—at least in part—to her approach of enthusing people to give art a chance. She built this approach in her master thesis (Groot, 1997), for which she borrowed from positive psychology and Csikszentmihalyi's flow experience theory (1990). This theory refers to the experiences of intrinsically motivated people, engaged in an activity chosen for its own sake rather than as means to an end. Groot values the participants for their talents, takes their taste in music as the point of departure, and makes sure that the challenges she sets for the participants match their skills. The ensuing positive experiences, possibly even flow, make the participants want to continue going. Bos further elaborates on positive experiences through music in chapter 6 (see also Bos, 2015). Here it is important to note that letting migrants decide for themselves how they want to be represented and what they like to perform is less self-evident than it may seem. It increasingly contrasted with the national debate at the time, in which diversity in the arts was often interpreted as a threat to artistic quality and to the high standards of the established arts organisations. At least, that was what these organisations presented as their main concern regarding the new cultural diversity policy.

> "The seniors loved the attention, and even more, liked being approached as talented people..."

Groot's approach was a striking one, too, in a period in which the language used by the right wing (populist) opposition and public opinion became more openly exclusionary and outspoken with regard to the—in their opinion: failed—integration of (Muslim) migrants into Dutch society (e.g., Scheffer, 2000). Even though cultural policy was still brimming with good intentions with regard to diversity, the explicit and Eurocentric call for assimilation sounded ever louder. This call had been intermittently expressed from the early 1990s onwards by politicians such as Frits Bolkestein (1997) and Pim Fortuyn (1997) as well as by publicists such as Paul Scheffer (2000) and Paul Schnabel (2000). The call for migrants' assimilation into "Dutch national culture and identity" signified a move away from working towards multicultural, "salad bowl," or other models of society that allow migrants more space to define their cultural position in the host society (see Trienekens, 2004, p. 101).

A Changing Political Climate
After Rotterdam Cultural Capital 2001, Groot continued working in Rotterdam with a new edition of the Euro+ Songfestival programme. But the positive spirit in which the city had been willing to showcase its diverse population was soon to change abruptly. First, the attacks on the Pentagon in Washington and the World Trade Centre in New York on September 11, 2001, negatively influenced the diversity and integration debate in many Western societies, including the Netherlands. Second, the assassination of the Dutch right-wing politician Pim Fortuyn, in Rotterdam in spring 2002, and his party's landslide victory at the local elections soon thereafter, created havoc in Rotterdam politics. This was the first time a populist party made it to power in the Netherlands. The consequences were felt across the political spectrum and also reached the field of publicly funded arts. Local political and public support for cultural diversity policies diminished, as did support for the arts in general, understood by populist politicians as a "leftist hobby."

The year 2002 signalled not only the premature end of the national "Dutch third way" political coalition, but also of the positive approach to diversity in national cultural policy. Preparations for the national cultural policy period 2005-2008 were already advancing and showed that cultural diversity policy would become substituted with the more generic concept of "social cohesion" (OC&W, 2003a; OC&W, 2003b). With tension rising between Muslim and non-Muslim citizens, the then secretary of state for culture celebrated the "binding potential" of the arts. She recognised this potential especially within the domain of cultural heritage:

Cultural heritage is the material basis of our shared culture and history. (...) Knowledge of our cultural heritage contributes to a cultural self-awareness that is indispensible in a multicultural society. In this added value to society lies the justification for supporting the arts and culture (OC&W, 2003a, p. 2).

Thus began a period of national navel-gazing with, e.g., heated debates around the construction of the national (cultural) history canon, and later on, a national history museum. The extent to which the cultural heritage of the various migrant groups was included, or rather, the question of how to archive the new joined cultural heritage that was being built in everyday life in the meantime, was not effectively addressed.

In hindsight, we can conclude that the policy objectives, for the period 2005-2008, were largely utilitarian: the arts as a meeting ground for polarised societal groups. Although that is certainly one of the arts' strengths, the policy shift had a detrimental effect on the location of diversity in the arts. For it meant, above all, that policy's incentives and earmarked budgets aimed at stimulating culturally diverse artistic productions and at increasing diversity in programming and among audiences of established cultural venues were largely scaled down. Also, the national Action Plan Cultural Diversity was dismantled and not extended into the new policy period. With regard to the integration discourse, the tone of the debate deteriorated even further. Specifically, in Rotterdam, the populist right-wing city council suggested some wild ideas such as erecting a "cordon sanitaire" around the city to prevent more people with a migration background from moving to Rotterdam or the dispersal of migrant households more evenly among the local boroughs. If implemented, such measures would have had serious implications for the freedom and equal rights of migrants and their households.

The Introduction to Intergenerationality

The altered political context burdened Groot's work with Rotterdam's migrant seniors. In 2005, however, Groot could unexpectedly take another distinctive step in the development of her music programme. As part of the Rotterdam Koorts (Fever) Festival, the Euro+ migrant senior talents were invited to a musical encounter with the young talents of two Rotterdam talent development programmes: "Talent2Star" and "Habibi Mahgribi." Watching the combined concert made Groot realize that this was the kind of energy both the seniors and her team were looking for. And, as soon became apparent, the young people did too. Children are presumed to have ample knowledge of the musical roots of their (grand)parents, but Groot experienced that this is often not the case. The youngsters attending the program not only learned a lot about the music of their parents and families, they relished the attention and recognition their family members and cultural roots received. Groot realized then that the young people suffer because of society's predominantly negative perception of migrant seniors—portraying them as a problem instead of how the young people see them: as strong, courageous people who had the guts to migrate in order to build a new life for themselves and their families in an unknown, foreign country.

Consequently, even though the choice to work in an intergenerational manner may not have been a preconceived or deliberate methodological one, the energy it set free has determined the way in which Groot works ever since. This early discovery of the power of intergenerational work makes Groot a pioneer and her projects an avant-garde practice within the Dutch cultural field. Because, even though cultural policy had begun to acknowledge the social-cohesive qualities of the arts, the exchange was rather crudely envisioned to take place between ethnic groups: between, e.g., the "Turks," the "Moroccans," etc. and the "Dutch." Intergenerational exchange was not discussed in the realm of cultural policy; super-diversity was still far from policy's understanding of people's identities.

"This early discovery of the power of intergenerational work makes Groot a pioneer and her projects an avant-garde..."

Loud and Soft Voices

Hence, from 2005 onward, cultural diversity, age, and "intergenerationality" formed the basis of Groot's programmes. Between 2005 and 2009, Groot continued working in this manner, assisted from 2007 by music director Paul Mayer. His background in both psychology and music turned out to be ideal for what the music programme tries to achieve: to get the best out of the individual participants, to build a strong group and to reach a high musical standard.

Their intergenerational work was supported by Netwerk CS, i.e., a tiny national organisation commissioned in 2001 by the secretary of state for culture to advance cultural diversity in the Dutch cultural sector. Whereas Netwerk CS was appreciative of the intergenerational element in their approach, at the time, Groot experienced this to be far less the case with other funding bodies. Groot's foundation suffered several—as she calls it—"near-death experiences" during that period.

In the meantime, at the national policy level, an interesting discrepancy became manifest. On the one hand, the then secretary of state for culture, as opposed to his predecessors, explicitly refrained from prescribing the cultural sector what to do with regard to diversity (OC&W, 2007). On the other hand, the Council for Culture (Raad voor Cultuur), the ministry's advisory body, continued to draw attention to diversity issues and even proposed a more complex interpretation of diversity than the usual one-dimensional reference to a person's ethnicity. In its report *To Innovate, To Participate!* (RvC, 2007), the Council suggested the substitution of the term "diversity" with "cultural citizenship" to express the growing importance of cultural practices to society at large and the increased interlacing of politics, the economy, and culture. Cultural citizenship additionally hinted at the need to improve citizenship skills to better prepare citizens to deal with the contemporary complexity of society. However laudable the attempt to launch a more complex understanding of diversity, by the Council for Culture as well as Netwerk CS, MusicGenerations and other small initiatives, the political climate did not provide the fertile ground it needed to become effective. In the Netherland and in Rotterdam, diversity by then was predominantly debated with reference to integration (assimilation). This debate was further obstructed by right-wing populist politicians' persistent conflation of the presence of Muslims in the Netherlands with terrorism and Muslim-extremism, even more so after terrorist attacks on public transport in London on July 7, 2005. All in all, there was no room for the introduction of a more advanced concept of diversity into Dutch policies or the public debate at the time. The loud voices once again shouted down the soft ones.

Adding Faith to the Mix

In 2009, Kosmopolis Rotterdam offered Groot the opportunity to develop an interreligious programme: "In Choir." Groot got together several Rotterdam choirs from different religions and generations. The set-up was largely the same as in its previous programmes: rehearsals, separate small concerts by a few choirs, followed by a collective final concert. A questionnaire (Trienekens, 2011, p. 68) among the participants showed that this programme provided a platform for contact and exchange that almost half of the respondents believed would otherwise not have happened. Additionally, almost 50 per cent of the respondents indicated that their participation in the programme made them appreciate and understand other religions better. At rehearsals, participants had dinner together, and discussed their religious similarities and differences. The programme's biggest challenge proved to be reaching a common agreement among the religious choir leaders regarding the lyrics of the songs. The objective of the programme was to have the choirs sing not only their own religious repertoire, but also that of other religions as well as newly composed songs. It regularly proved necessary to alter the lyrics in such a way that all faith communities could recognise themselves in them. With Groot's mediation, the religious choir leaders found a way to collaborate and perform together.

Interestingly, in this programme, religion could function as a unifying concept, whereas at the time, religion had already become the main marker of difference among people. By then, as Lucassen (2005) illustrated, the Muslim faith had become commonly represented as non-compatible with the values of Judeo-Christian tradition. Lucassen

(2005, p. 3-4) dates the emergence of religious and cultural markers over colour and race back to the Islamic revolution under Ayatollah Khomeini in Iran in 1979, which culminated in the Rushdie affair in 1989, and the First Gulf War against Iraq a few years later. This shift in attention, which occurred throughout Western Europe, coincided with family-reunification migration to Western Europe of migrants from Muslim countries such as Turkey, Morocco, Algeria, and Tunisia. The confluence of changes in the international political climate and the actual settlement of people from Muslim countries, who became highly visible through the establishment of mosques and Islamic dress code, led to the widespread view that the presence of Islamic migrants is problematic. It also led to the belief that the values of these migrants are fundamentally opposed to Judeo-Christian tradition and the heritage of the enlightenment, such as equality between men and women and separation of church and state. The events of September 11, 2001, as well as the ensuing "war on terrorism," further strengthened the conviction that the culture of Islam and that of the West are irreconcilable. "In Choir," nonetheless, showed that, even though the different participants did not understand or interpret religion in the same way, they recognised that religion itself was equally important to them all. In spite of differences between religious convictions, age, and ethnic backgrounds, the act of believing represented a shared value. Groot's tested approach—inviting a myriad of people to join her programmes based on their love of music—took the sting out of an otherwise polarising practice.

A Changing Cultural (Funding) Climate

At the national level, cultural policy during the period 2009-2012 was absorbed in redesigning the structurally funded cultural infrastructure, and to a lesser extent, in promoting innovation and cultural participation (OC&W, 2007). Even before this cultural policy period had come to an end, the national government announced massive cutbacks in national spending in several fields such as care, welfare, and the arts, to become effective January 1, 2013.

In the meantime, Rotterdam's populist local government formulated its policy for the new cultural period, adopting the national policy approach to the cohesive quality of the arts: "Who takes notice of their own and other people's cultures, opens oneself up to other people and to oneself" (GR, 2007, p. 40; cf. OC&W, 2012, p. 3). To increase cultural participation in the new policy period, extra support would be given to small-scale cultural initiatives around amateur art and community art (GR, 2007, p. 11). In 2009, moreover, Rotterdam would be Youth Capital of Europe. The programme focused on expressing the culture and talents of Rotterdam's diverse youth; it left little room for intergenerational bridging.

As on the national level, Rotterdam's next policy period, 2013-2016, was dominated by drastic budget cuts. The result was an even tighter link between the arts and the economic, spatial, and social priorities on the city agenda (GR, 2012, p. 5; RRKC, 2015, p. 26). In this respect, the policy paper clearly expresses the diminished general support for the arts as such. Arguments for public support of the arts are almost entirely formulated in instrumental terms (GR, 2012, p. 6–8): policy aimed at cultural entrepreneurship and demanded that cultural organisations take social responsibility and engage more directly with their urban surroundings. Talent development continued to be a policy target, grounded in the belief that the arts contribute to the broad development of children and young people. The third target was the arts' contribution to a lively city (centre): to make Rotterdam more attractive as a place to visit or live and more economically viable. The changes in the local climate for the arts are also manifest in the formulation of the target groups for cultural policy: children and young people. Anyone above 25 years of age, who wanted to participate in the arts, would have to pay "the full price." This echoes the right-wing populist claim that public arts funding only serves the already well-to-do and higher-educated. Although statistics show that this claim holds true for audiences of classical music, ballet, and the like (Kraaykamp et al., 2010), it ignores the large group of older Rotterdammers living on tiny budgets. It also ignores the prerequisite for social mobility: diverse networks in terms of age and socio-economic status.

Moving Beyond National Borders

The Rotterdam cultural department rejected Groot's application for structural funding for the cultural policy period 2009-2012. Whereas the city in which Groot had been working from the very beginning did not want to support MusicGenerations financially, luckily the national Fund for Cultural Participation did grant Groot's foundation structural, i.e. 4-year, funding for this period. In the next cultural policy period, 2013-2016, the Rotterdam cultural council followed suit. In this regard, MusicGenerations' programmes did not suffer too much under the new cultural policy regime. In recent years, moreover, Groot's foundation has successfully applied for support from other public and private funds, such as Prins Bernhard Cultuurfonds, VSB Fonds, RCOAK, and Rotterdam Festivals. Furthermore, in 2013, a national programme on age and cultural participation was launched, called "Long Live Arts." Although the recent policy attention for seniors, art, and wellbeing underscores and supports Groot's focus on age, it falls short of implementing an intergenerational perspective on cultural production and participation. Notwithstanding such shortcomings in policy and funding, the funding allocated to MusicGenerations allowed Groot and Mayer to continue working in

Rotterdam and other Dutch cities. Additionally, the funding facilitated MusicGenerations programmes in other European Capitals of Cultural, as well as in, for instance, the Ruhr area, Istanbul in 2010 (the then Cultural Capital of Europe), Ankara and East-Turkey in 2012 (celebration of 400 years of Turkish-Dutch relations), and the return to the Kurdish areas of Turkey in 2013. The work in the Dersim region, East Turkey, in 2012 and 2013, was the source of inspiration for the Talent for Freedom-programme that Groot's team began in 2014 in the Netherlands (Groot, 2013, p. 32).

From Diversity to Super-Diversity

Both the national and international experiences brought Groot's team new insights into what working with diversity and age in the arts entails and it further broadened their interpretation of diversity to super-diversity. The insight that diversity is about much more than just ethnicity or nationality was obviously brought about by international developments such as wars and natural disasters that subsequently changed the composition of the group of migrants arriving in the Netherlands to a myriad of ethnicities, nationalities, as well as social-economic backgrounds, ages, and immigration statuses. A more complex understanding of diversity was further obtained from their participants, whom Groot's team saw moving in and out of contexts of diversity and operating in multiple layers of identification (cf. Arnaut, 2012, p.4). This became apparent in simple statements such as "I may be from Indonesia, but I'd rather sing jazz." Chapter 10 further details the identity-lessons that can be learned from the practice of MusicGenerations.

"I may be from Indonesia, but I'd rather sing jazz."

The participants and the international exchanges, additionally, also provided the team with deeper insight into the different forms of repression. At home, one participant wrote "So One Dai" about the slave history of his family. The two trips to the Kurdish-Turkish areas highlighted the privilege of being able to sing in one's own language—something the Kurds, to this day, are not allowed to do as the recent imprisonment of several Kurdish singers by the Turkish authorities illustrates (e.g., Corporate Watch, 2015).

MusicGenerations' increasingly complex understanding of the role of ethnicity in people's identities continued to contrast with public discourse. An analysis of newspaper coverage of the period 1995-2005 reveals a shift in concerns associated with migrants and their children (see Essed & Trienekens, 2008, p. 62). In 1995, the main concerns were political (legislation, etc.) and discrimination. In 1999, attention turned to criminality and the issue of asylum seekers. In 2002, the main topics were criminality, cultural differences and integration. In 2005, cultural differences and integration remained the main themes, but were complemented by articles on Muslim extremism.

Were we to extend the analysis, the concerns we would discern in recent years would at least be the polarization between societal groups and the alleged negative consequences of spatial segregation (this can also be shown by the amount of research on this topic commissioned in recent years, see Ponds et al., 2015). Additionally, the concerns with the risk of radicalization among young Dutch-Muslims and with Muslim extremism will have remained topical as a consequence of the attacks on Charlie Hebdo in January, on several locations in Paris in November 2015, and of various attacks of IS in several countries in the Middle East. Since 2015, we can be sure that the number of articles on refugees has also vastly increased.

Political discourse also increasingly took on ever more exclusionary traits. Across Europe, the populist right-wing voice has become louder. In the Netherlands, this voice is personified by Geert Wilders, populist right-wing politician of the "Party for Freedom." Wilders explicitly distinguishes between the "Dutch" and "others." In 2007, he argued that members of parliament should not be allowed a bi-national status (two passports). Among his current statements is his wish to "close the Dutch border and refusing all refugees, including Middle-Eastern Christian refugees" (RD.nl, 2016). His critique on Islam, immigration, the European Union, the arts, and the political left gained him popularity among a large portion of the electorate; in the 2010 national election, he received 15.5 per cent of the votes. Like other populist parties, Wilders exploits popular sentiments that Heijne (2012, p. 8) summarizes as:

Taxpayers feel that they are paying for other people whilst they themselves are increasingly being used and ignored. From this perspective, multiculturalism as an ideology, the subsidizing of art and nature, and development cooperation are seen as expressions of misplaced superiority, as means by which a privileged class can feel superior to others at the expense of the "common citizen."

For his claim to be able to put a stop to all this, Wilders may well be rewarded with a premiership in the 2017 national elections.

A Divided Society

For now, we will have to wait and see how official migration and integration politics in Europe and the Netherlands will be affected by the large numbers of refugees currently arriving in Europe, by the attacks in Paris, or the New Year's Eve assaults in Cologne—and by everything that is bound to happen before and after publication of this volume. We will also have to wait and see if society will become even more divided. Will the current gap increase between those people who take to the streets against the accommodation of refugees and those who do the same in defence of their arrival? Between those who passionately defend "Zwarte Piet" as an innocent Dutch cultural tradition and the increasing number of people who have come to realise that it is an offensive practice? A nuanced debate is still hard to find: it is either portrayed as all bad or all good. A reality check may be helpful (cf. Žižek, 2016) as well as an inclusion of the people concerned in the debates.

Divided is also the image with regard to inclusion in various societal domains. For instance, a few prominent positions of influence—such as the Speaker of the Dutch House of Representatives and the mayor of Rotterdam, the Netherlands' second city—are occupied by Moroccan-Dutch. But the boards of institutes for higher education and other (semi) public organisations and enterprises remain predominantly white. There are more and more columnists of colour writing for Dutch newspapers, but papers still refuse to abandon use of the word "allochtoon" (cf. Özdil, 2015, p. 86). These are just two examples to illustrate that there has been progress, but important as this is, it remains piecemeal.

Future Opportunities for MusicGenerations?

In addition to international musical exchanges, Groot continued producing MusicGenerations in the Netherlands, aimed at bridging social divisions. In 2012-2013, the programme was called "Now or Never," and in 2014-2015, "Talent for Freedom." Before venturing out into new themes and domains, i.e., the accommodation and integration of refugees, Groot seeks to hand over the heritage of almost 15 years of intergenerational talent development—the music programme and the approach—to local cultural and social organisations throughout the Netherlands. So far, it has not always proven to be easy. Groot has experienced that certain Dutch cities and geographical areas are more receptive to the intergenerational and super-diversity approach than others.

> Groot seeks to hand over the heritage of almost 15 years of intergenerational talent development—the music programme and the approach—to local cultural and social organisations throughout the Netherlands.

Its future opportunities are also related to the question if MusicGenerations' core concepts of (super)diversity and intergenerationality will better connect to cultural policy and funding objectives in the future than in the past. Let us briefly speculate on the extent to which this might be the case. Like the divided image sketched above for society at large, for the cultural sector, too, we have to conclude that "yes, there has been progress, but there is still a lot left to achieve." Take the diversification of audiences. The literature presents us with a contradictory image. Positive research findings are presented by, e.g., Planbureau voor de Leefomgeving (2014, p. 85–86), which found that the cultural background of audiences in urban areas has become more diverse. On a less positive note, the Council for Culture discerns the development in which young people (RvC, 2014, p. 35) and "an increasing group of people from non-western background lack a connection to traditional 'canonized' cultural expressions" (RvC, 2015, p. 59). The Rotterdam Council for Art and Culture (RRKC, 2015, p. 20) appears to combine these two findings as it discerns a geographical disparity between local boroughs and the city centre: a diverse audience in local cultural centres (LCCs) and a far "whiter" audience in central theatres and museums. I think it is safe to state that, in spite of positive change in certain cultural and geographical areas, work still needs to be done to make the publicly funded cultural sector more representative of society. Still more cultural initiatives, based on an elaborate perspective of generations and diversity, are required to make an enhanced understanding of diversity in the public cultural sector more commonplace.

In this context, the highly upbeat tone of the Rotterdam cultural policy paper for the period 2017-2020 (GR, 2015) is also worth mentioning. It differs from previous papers in that it has been written in collaboration with established cultural organisations and local cultural entrepreneurs. The paper expresses the wish to establish a more dynamic, creative, and flexible cultural sector. This should be a sector that bridges gaps between established and new cultural initiatives or artistic expressions and between different groups: between old and young, rich and poor, and people from different cultures and ethnicities. The policy paper also mentions the city's transnational ties:

Who is to draw a line between Rotterdam and each country that is represented here, ends up looking at an impressive web of lines. The whole world is at home in Rotterdam. Arts and culture should mirror this cosmopolitan atmosphere and use it to its advantage. (GR, 2015, p. 5).

Although this latest policy paper takes a stance regarding diversity, and fleetingly alludes to building intergenerational bridges, the question remains whether initiatives such as MusicGenerations sufficiently fit the type of hyped, trendy cultural pop-up, design or festival projects the policy paper predominantly describes and the cultural department apparently seeks to support. Also nationally, as the Council for Culture points out (RvC, 2015, p. 62), small-scale, cross-disciplinary, and culturally diverse initiatives continue to fall between two stools when they apply for public funding.

At the national level, talent development is one of the five main objectives of cultural policy for the period 2017-2020. The focus is, however, either on talent development of *young* people (cultural education and youth theatre groups) or on initiatives in the structurally funded cultural infrastructure dealing with talent development of *professional* artists (OC&W, 2015). The national programme Long Live Arts focused on cultural participation of older people. Some projects funded through this programme had an intergenerational element in which the older and younger generation were an indirect inspiration to one another. But most projects did not start from the structural collaboration based on equality between the generations, nor from the cultural diversity that characterises MusicGenerations. Long Live Arts, moreover, comes to an end in 2016. At this point, it is unclear to what extent the theme will remain on the national agenda. What is clear is that it has not triggered more attention for intergenerationality, super-diversity, or intersectionality for that matter, in the national government's vision on talent development or on participation in the arts.

At the national level, cultural policy now formulates the arts' power to connect as the "social value of the arts" (in addition to its intrinsic and economic value). This value is to be expressed in collaboration between the arts and other sectors such as care, welfare, or industry. Due to the consequences of the massive budget cuts, the ministry for culture acknowledges the need for stronger profiling among cultural institutions and allows these institutions more freedom to define their profiles. Euphemisms as "one cultural institution may choose an international profile, another may venture out into local boroughs" (OC&W, 2015, p. 9) seem to sum up both the ministry's vision on profiling and on diversity and may be too noncommittal.

At the same time, however, the policy paper's short paragraph on cultural diversity is translated into the objective to check the implementation of the Code Cultural Diversity by the structurally funded cultural infrastructure—a code that the ministry additionally wants to acknowledge in the Code Governance Culture (OC&W, 2015, p. 16–17). The Code Cultural Diversity is also mentioned in some of the policy papers of the national cultural funds (see FPK, 2016, p. 18). The Code Cultural Diversity encompasses the question of diversity among staff. This is an urgent matter given the vast discrepancy, as the Council for Culture pointed out (2015, p. 61), between the cultural and ethnic composition of the programme as well as the staff of publicly funded arts organisations and the make-up of our main cities' population, i.e., around half of the people living in the largest Dutch cities have a history of migration. There seems indeed to be a debate emerging in the cultural sector on diversity among staff (e.g., Welingelichte Kringen, 2015). Linking the Code and the issue of a representative staff to governance—i.e., to achieve diversity also among the higher echelons of cultural organisations, not just among staff—can be considered progress, because these issues were more or less cast aside in the previous policy periods.

Saved by the Council?
In its latest advice to the Ministry of Culture, the Council for Culture further extends its diversity thinking (RvC, 2015, p. 60–61). It writes that, for the longest time, cultural

policy applied the term "diversity" to people of non-Western backgrounds and functioned as an isolated topic in cultural policy. The Council states that, in our current society, the term needs to refer to differences in taste, backgrounds, and frames of reference of the various groups that make up society. "Diversity" as a concept should therefore not just encompass ethnic diversity, but also gender, economic, and social diversity. The Council also discerns the need for new vocabulary to be able to constructively discuss (cultural) diversity in the years to come. Will the Council for Culture succeed in being heard this time? The following three chapters, at least, contribute to the development of a new vocabulary and an enhanced understanding of—what in this chapter continued to be called—"cultural diversity."

> "Diversity" as a concept should therefore not just encompass ethnic diversity, but also gender, economic, and social diversity.

Change will inevitably come, because the simple fact is that the Dutch population is a majority-minority one. The question is how fast things will change. For the past 15 years, we can cautiously conclude that progress has been made, but is has been slow, piecemeal, and not yet far-reaching enough. And even though currently things may look up a bit—i.e., the Council for Culture continues to put the issue of cultural diversity on the agenda and there are signs of a re-emerging debate on the issue of diversity in the cultural sector—we should not get our hopes up too high. If the Netherlands ends up with a populist right-wing government after the 2017 national elections, not just the issue of cultural diversity, but the whole cultural sector will have to prepare itself for another blow.

Tonia

References

Arnaut, K. (2012). Super-diversity: elements of an emerging perspective. *Diversities*, 14(2), 1-17.

Bolkestein, F. (1997). *Moslim in de polder*. Amsterdam/Antwerpen: Uitgeverij Contact.

Bos, E. (2012). *Beleid voor cultuur en migranten: Rijksbeleid en uitvoeringspraktijk 1980-2004*. Amsterdam: SWP.

Bos, E. (2015). *Twee oren en een mond*. Lectorale rede Hogeschool van Amsterdam.

Corporate Watch. (2015, August 27). Imprisoned for singing in Kurdish: Support Nûdem Durak. https://corporatewatch.org/news/2015/aug/27/imprisoned-singing-kurdish-support-n%C3%BBdem-durak on 19 February 2016.

COS. (2011). *Bevolking van Rotterdam naar land van nationaliteit*, op 1-1-2001 t/m 2011. Rotterdam: Centrum voor Onderzoek en Statistiek, 29-04-11 (D05)

Csikszentmihalyi, M. (1990). Flow: The Psychology of Optimal Experience. New York: HarperCollins.

Essed, Ph. & Trienekens, S. (2008). Who wants to feel white? Race, Dutch culture and contested identities. *Ethnic and Racial Studies*, 31(1), 52–72.

FPK – Fonds Podiumkunsten. (2015). *Beleidsplan 2017-2020: Vitale Verbindingen*. Den Haag: Fonds Podiumkunsten.

Fortuyn, P. (1997). *Tegen de islamisering van onze cultuur*. Amsterdam: A.W. Bruna Uitgevers.

GR – Gemeente Rotterdam. (2007). In verbeelding van elkaar samen het toneel van stad zijn: *Uitgangspunten voor het cultuurbeleid 2009-2012*. Rotterdam: Dienst Kunst en Cultuur, Gemeente Rotterdam.

GR – Gemeente Rotterdam. (2012). *Midden in de stad: Het Rotterdamse Cultuurplan 2013-2016*. Rotterdam: Dienst Kunst en Cultuur, Gemeente Rotterdam.

GR – Gemeente Rotterdam. (2015). *Reikwijdte & armslag: Uitgangspuntennota voor het Rotterdamse Cultuurplan 2017–2020*. Rotterdam: Dienst Kunst en Cultuur, Gemeente Rotterdam.

Groot, C. (1997). *The Art of Seeing* (Unpublished master's thesis). University of Amsterdam.

Groot, C. (2013). *Music Generations 2013: Bestuursverslag Stichting Euro+ Songfestival*. Rotterdam: Euro+ Songfestival.

Heijne, B. (2012). *Development Cooperation, Humanism, Crisis - Where to from here?* Published December 2012 by the Knowledge Programme. Den Haag: Hivos.

Kraaykamp, G., Eijck, K. van, & Ultee, W. (2010). Status, class and culture in the Netherlands. In T. Wing Chan (Ed.), *Social Status and Cultural Consumption* (pp. 169–203). Cambridge: Cambridge University Press.

Lucassen, L. (2005). *The Immigrant Threat*. Champaign, IL: University of Illinois Press.

OC&W. (1999a). *Ruim Baan voor Culturele Diversiteit*, mei 1999. Zoetermeer: Ministerie van Onderwijs, Cultuur en Wetenschappen.

OC&W. (1999b). *Cultuur als Confrontatie: Uitgangspunten voor het cultuurbeleid 2001-2004*. Zoetermeer: Ministerie van Onderwijs, Cultuur en Wetenschappen.

OC&W. (2002). *Cultuurbeleid in Nederland*. Zoetermeer: Ministerie van Onderwijs, Cultuur en Wetenschappen.

OC&W. (2003a). *Uitgangspuntenbrief Cultuur*. Den Haag: Ministerie van Onderwijs, Cultuur en Wetenschappen.
OC&W. (2003b). Meer dan de som: Beleidsbrief Cultuur 2004-2007. Den Haag: Ministerie van Onderwijs, Cultuur en Wetenschappen.

OC&W. (2007). *Kunst van Leven: hoofdlijnen cultuurbeleid*. Den Haag: Ministerie van Onderwijs, Cultuur en Wetenschap.

OC&W. (2012). *Cultuur beweegt. De betekenis van cultuur in een veranderende samenleving*. Tweede Kamer, vergaderjaar 2012-2013, nr. 32820-76.

OC&W. (2015). *Ruimte voor cultuur. Uitgangspunten cultuurbeleid 2017-2020*. Den Haag: Ministerie van Onderwijs, Cultuur en Wetenschap.

Özdil, Z. (2015). *Nederland mijn Vaderland*. Amsterdam: De Bezige Bij.

Planbureau voor de Leefomgeving (2014). *Balans van de Leefomgeving 2014: De toekomst is nú*. Den Haag: PBL.

Ponds, R., Ham, M. van, & Marlet, G. (2015). *Verschillen, ongelijkheid en segregatie*. Utrecht: Atlas voor Gemeenten.

RD.nl. (2016) Wilders: *Grens óók dicht voor christelijke vluchteling*. In Reformatorisch Dagblad, 11-02-2016. Consulted on 22 February 2016.

RvC – Raad voor Cultuur. (2002). *Adviesaanvraag publieksbereik hedendaagse beeldende kunst/musea: Antwoord aan de staatssecretaris*. Den Haag: Raad voor Cultuur.

RvC – Raad voor Cultuur. (2007). *Innoveren, Participeren! Advies agenda cultuurbeleid en culturele basisinfrastructuur*. Den Haag: Raad voor Cultuur.

RvC – Raad voor Cultuur. (2014). *Cultuurverkenning: Ontwikkelingen en trends in het culturele leven in Nederland*. Den Haag: Raad voor cultuur.

RvC – Raad voor Cultuur. (2015). *Agenda Cultuur 2017-2020 en verder*. Den Haag: Raad voor cultuur.

Richards, G., Hitters, E., & Fernandes, C. (2002). *Rotterdam and Porto Cultural Capitals 2001: Visitor research*. Arnhem: ATLAS, 67.

Rijpma, S. et al. (2000). Diversiteit in vrijetijdsbesteding. Rotterdam: COS.
RRKC. (2015). Sectoranalyse. Rotterdam: Rotterdamse Raad voor Kunst en Cultuur.

Scheffer, P. (2000, January 20). *Het multiculturele drama*. NRC Handelsblad, p. 6.

Schnabel, P. (2000). *De multiculturele illusie*. Utrecht: Forum.

Trienekens, S. (2004). *Urban paradoxes: Lived citizenship and the position of diversity in the arts*. Amsterdam: Trienekens.

Trienekens, S. (2011). *Wrikken aan Beeldvorming*. Rotterdam: Kosmopolis Rotterdam.

Welingelichte Kringen. (2015, December 17). *Filmfonds moet zelf ook diverser worden*. Welingelichte Kringen.

Žižek, S. (2016, January 13). *The Cologne attacks were an obscene version of carnival*. NewStatesman. http://www.newstatesman.com/world/europe/2016/01/slavoj-zizek-cologne-attacks

2010
Istanbul

2011
Now or Never

2012
Kurdish parts of Turkey

2013
Kurdish parts of Turkey

2014 / 2015
Talent for freedom

2015
Age Included
Conference

2015
Age Included
Conference

2015
Age Included
Conference

8. All Included?

Zihni Özdil

Exclusion

In the past few years, the Netherlands has had a revival in its public debate of themes related to exclusion. Ethnic discrimination, homophobia, Islamophobia, anti-Semitism, and feminism are back on the societal agenda, even though some are not very fond of this development.

Somewhat underplayed is the question of age. When I told friends that I was asked to contribute to *Age Included* and write about how age relates to diversity, they automatically assumed it would be only about senior citizens. That is quite an interesting phenomenon: when we talk about age, we mostly think only about the elderly.

In itself, that is quite understandable: the Netherlands is a rapidly aging country. The "elderly market" is becoming more important every day (see, for example, the political party 50+ or the popular TV station Omroep MAX). This volume deals with seniority, but also with much more, since exclusion on the basis of age is something young people experience as well.

Euphemisms

The success of the labour union campaign *Young & United*, which focuses on underpayment of young adult workers, shows that the so-called participation society—the Dutch euphemism for the dismantling of the welfare state—will be an important theme on both sides of the age spectrum. The elderly are becoming poorer and youth is becoming more "flexible," another interesting term. When it comes to interesting terms, perhaps we should guard against euphemisms such as "super-diversity" and "dynamic interaction" in this volume as well.

Pointing out the complexity of diversity is, of course, important; however, the reality remains that people tend to segregate more and more—not only physically but especially mentally—in Western European societies, especially the Netherlands. While the middle class is slowly eroding, the gap between the haves and have-nots is increasing. This class segregation is crossed with ethnic segregation. Within ethnic minorities, there is always a small segment that is "doing well" when it comes to education or the labour market, but even most of those "who do well" tend to segregate ethnically outside the workplace.

Super-apartheid

Ethnic segregation is also connected to age segregation. The 2010 young mayor of the London borough of Lewisham, Jakob Sakil, pointed out that the super-diverse inhabitants of his neighbourhood live segregated from one another. The same pattern is discernable in Dutch cities. White Dutch who live in those neighbourhoods, whether older generations who remained or young "hipsters" dwelling in gentrified parts, do not mix with residents of colour. Would it therefore not be more precise to call the complexity of diversity in our society "super-apartheid"? The term "super-diversity"—despite the meaning academics may attach to it—sounds all too positive to the general public.

Why are we, especially some of us academics, inclined to assume that diversity, or difference, and mixing contradict each other? Would not mixing, not only physically, but also mentally, be a better perspective to take on the, to put it subtly, ever expanding *clusterfuck* of neoliberalism and right-wing populism? Would we not all win if older and younger people, white people and people of colour, LGBTs and heterosexuals, abled and disabled people were to mix together?

Mixing

One thing I am sure of is that, if we seriously want to fight the problem of institutional racism and segregation, we need to establish a cultural shift towards a country in which Dutch people of colour are truly considered part of the Dutch, i.e., considered as Dutch as any other Dutch person. New Dutch citizenship is thus not about tolerance, multiculturalism, "integration," or any other concept that keeps dividing "them" from "us," but about inclusive nationalism: you are one of us and that is the way it remains. We will also have to understand that there is no "own culture" of Dutch people of colour. This culture is also by definition Dutch, comparable to the specific cultures of people in the various Dutch regions. We can continue to differ in opinion on all kinds of important matters, but no longer in the context of "we true Dutch" versus "them." This cultural shift is urgently needed, because our young people have already internalised the Dutch segregation. They too use terminology such as "those Dutch" or "I will go back one day," to e.g., Turkey or Morocco, even though they were born in the Netherlands.

Facts show that encounters and debates among people of all colours as well as the acquisition of knowledge of, e.g., the history of slavery, are adequate instruments in raising such awareness, in triggering that cultural shift. New Dutch citizenship and inclusive nationalism thus demand that we mix much more. True integration is mixing: physically and social-culturally. Mixing is also debating discriminatory ideas together. Because, if "unknown" equals "unloved," then the reverse will also hold true.

9. Towards an Open Approach to Integration

Super-diversity, Intersectionality, and the Integration Context[1]

Maurice Crul

Introduction

The theoretical debate on assimilation and integration in the last two decades has been dominated by grand theories such as segmented assimilation theory and the newly-articulated assimilation theory by Alba and Nee. The theories served to explain assimilation and integration processes, especially in the case of a clear majority group and a small number of sizable migrant groups. Both grand theories are based on empirical data comparing ethnic groups to each other and/or to the "white" majority population. With the growing diversity of immigrant groups and also the growing diversity within immigrant groups, in terms of differences both within the same generation as well as between generations, the ethnic group as a unit of analysis has become problematic. Can super-diversity theory fill in the gap between the grand theories and the changed reality?

I will argue that super-diversity theory can partially show us the way. To further build an alternative theoretical perspective, we also need to borrow from the perspective of intersectionality and the integration context theory. I will bring together the intersectional approach in super-diversity theory that promotes looking at multidimensional aspects of agency with insights from the integration context theory that emphasises the importance of national institutional arrangements. Such a re-formulated super-diversity theory stresses the need to look at within-groups differences in relation to differences in the local and national contexts. It promotes studying the interlocking relationship between the impact of different background characteristics and the differences in opportunities that different local and national contexts offer, with the aim of developing an international comparative theory suited to studying the new reality of our cities. As such, it facilitates a more open approach in which other possible axes of differences such as age cohorts, changes in gender roles, marriage patterns, or generation are also core elements and in which differences in institutional arrangements in school, the labour market, and child care (pre-school) are considered.

Grand Assimilation Theories and Their Shortcomings

American theories have been dominant across our field of study in the last two decades. This is especially true for the segmented assimilation theory (Portes & Zhou, 1993). This grand theory has helped us to make sense of different assimilation outcomes inter-generationally across different ethnic groups. The authors claim that some ethnic groups are socially mobile because of their strong social cohesion and resistance to Americanisation and argue that other ethnic groups assimilate into the poor black American underclass. The general idea of segmented assimilation is that ethnic groups as a whole follow one of the three typical patterns described in the theory: either two possible upward variants or one downward variant (Portes & Rumbaut, 2001). The emphasis in segmented assimilation theory is on ethnic and socio-economic characteristics of the first generation that influence the type and/or speed of assimilation pathways.

In their book *Remaking the American Mainstream*, Alba and Nee (2003) remodelled and updated classical assimilation theory, emphasizing that the main trend for all migrant groups in the USA is still assimilation into the mainstream over time. More recently, Alba summarizes his theoretical viewpoint in the following quote: "The social and cultural distance to the mainstream decreases, and life chances come to closely approximate those held by their peers in the dominant group, who are similar in socio-economic origin, birth cohort, and so forth" (Alba, Jimenéz, & Marrow, 2009, p. 449). There is a fair amount of consensus now about the newly-formulated assimilation theory's claim that there is more than one possible social mobility pathway, although it is disputed if entire ethnic groups can be fitted so neatly into one of the three segmented assimilation options (Waters, Tran, Kasinitz, & Mollenkopf, 2010).

The two mentioned American assimilation theories stem from an era in which the size of single ethnic minority groups was that big and the segregation of single ethnic minority groups was often so strong that this justified the talk about assimilation or integration on the ethnic group level. With the higher level of segregation in US cities, this theoretical frame was always more relevant in the USA than in Europe.

Both segmented and new assimilation theories describe social mobility as a linear process at the group level in which the assimilation progress is measured based on average outcomes at the group level. However, the growing diversity within ethnic groups makes this approach problematic. We need a more refined analysis that takes within-group differences into account. The ideas, practices, and goals within ethnic groups change over time, and as a result, the diversity within groups is often ample and it grows. Moreover, the new demography of cities and neighbourhoods without a clear-cut majority group creates a new situation for the children of both new and old migrant groups and of the old majority group. The old majority group is no longer the standard to which newcomers and children adapt. At the same time, there is no other dominant ethnic group in the majority-minority city. Many integration or assimilation situations are now characterised by a multiplicity of diversity in terms of the number of ethnic groups, the differences in generations, and socio-economic positions. This urges us to develop an approach that does not take ethnic groups as the primary unit of analysis. The term super-diversity presented itself as an appropriate concept for this context.

Super Diversity Theory and its Shortcomings

Steve Vertovec (2007) introduced the term super-diversity and used it to describe the increased diversity in ethnic groups now living in large Western European cities. Forty years ago, migrants to these cities came from a limited number of countries; nowadays from all over the world. Cities housing more than 170 nationalities are more the rule than the exception. Increased ethnic diversity alone is, however, not a solid argument to now add "super" to the established term diversity. So why should we consider using super-diversity instead? Blommaert and Maly (2014) argue that studying super-diversity stands for a higher level of analysis, superseding above and beyond single forms of diversity. The term alerts us to other axes of difference such as gender, education, age cohorts, and generations. Between and within ethnic groups, there is a growing difference between generations, between men and women, and between more and less educated people. This calls for a shift of focus from fixed entities such as "the ethnic group" to a dynamic interplay between different characteristics of individual members of ethnic groups and the fluid relationships between them; in other words, a shift from an "ethnic lens" to a multidimensional lens.

Scholars in the USA, where the framework of assimilation still pretty much kept its dominant position in the analyses of outcomes for migrants and their children, have hardly taken up the concept. In Europe, there is no similar dominance of one theoretical framework. This does not mean that super-diversity as a concept is uncritically adopted in Europe. For instance, the concept has been criticised for its conceptual vagueness and the lack of a clear definition of when to call a particular situation super-diverse (for an overview, see Meissner, 2015; Meissner & Vertovec, 2015). Another important critique is that super-diversity may describe a new reality, but does not provide a theoretical framework to explain differences in assimilation or integration outcomes.

The criticism of the conceptual vagueness of super-diversity, especially the lack of a clear definition of what exactly is considered to be a super-diverse city or neighbourhood, is fair critique. At what point does the increased diversification of ethnic groups become enough to apply the term super-diversity? In this article, I will apply a provisional and instrumental definition. I will only label cities and neighbourhoods as super-diverse when they present a majority-minority situation. The second characteristic of a super-diverse city or neighbourhood is that, in this majority-minority context, both the number and size of different ethnic groups must be substantial. These two criteria are based on the increased differentiation *between* ethnic groups. This is the most commonly used way to describe a situation as super-diverse in the literature (cf. Vertovec, 2007). I would add the importance of differences *within* ethnic groups, in terms of generation, gender, socio-economic status, religion, or age cohorts. Here super-diversity theory makes an important contribution: pointing out the need to include, next to ethnic background characteristics, other background characteristics in the analysis of, say, education, labour market, or housing outcomes.

Then there is the question if the urban reality has become so different that we really need a new theoretical framework? Rightly so, academics are very critical towards the introduction of new theories and concepts. Both grand theories— segmented assimilation theory and the newly-formulated assimilation theory by Alba and Nee—have been crucial in our understanding of processes of incorporation in two ways. The first way is in the understanding of the processes in which ethnic minority groups adapt to the majority group or the mainstream. The second way is in analysing the patterns of social mobility of different ethnic groups compared to each other and compared to the majority population. In this article, I will however show how in these two principal themes super-diversity theory can improve our understanding beyond the existing grand assimilation theories.

The Changed Reality and the Acknowledgement of Intersectionality

Many cities have become majority-minority cities. This first became a reality in North American cities such as New York, Los Angeles, and Toronto: cities that consist only of minorities. In these cities, there is no longer a dominant ethnic or racial majority group. Large Western European cities are moving very rapidly towards that same situation.

Amsterdam and Brussels recently became majority-minority cities

Amsterdam and Brussels recently became majority-minority cities. Considerable parts of London and Paris also are past the ethnic tipping point. Some describe this as "the diversity turn" or "the transition to diversity."

Another cardinal new trend in European cities is that classical migrant groups that came in the 1960s and 1970s as labour migrants now extend into three generations living in the city. Children and grandchildren of the first generation were mostly born in these very same cities and grew up there. They now form one of the established groups in the city. They are strongly rooted in the city, also because most of their close family lives there. People of native descent often come to the city to study and find work, and often leave again when they marry and start a family. This trend overthrows the picture of who are newcomers and who belong to the established group.

There is also an increasing diversity within diversity. Emerging patterns of social mobility in the second and third generations reveal large within-group differences that request from us a rethinking of the existing grand theories of assimilation. Within the second generation, we find big differences in educational and labour market outcomes. These differences increase within the third generation, resulting in polarisation within the same ethnic group and same generation.

Such trends challenge existing assimilation theories. The idea of assimilation or integration becomes, at any rate, more complex in a situation where there is no longer a clear majority group into which one is to assimilate or integrate. The pressure to assimilate, coming from the—old— majority group, is less strong if not backed by sheer numbers in everyday life. The group into which one assimilates in the concrete situation of a neighbourhood or a school is, as a result, more and more unlikely to be the old majority group, but rather an amalgam of people of different ethnic backgrounds, migration cohorts, migration statuses, and socio-economic positions. The polarisation of outcomes within ethnic groups makes it unrealistic to frame the position of people at the group level in ethnic terms primarily and challenges existing assimilation theories that predict a linear development over time at the group level.

This can, for instance, be shown by the representative TIES survey among second-generation Turks and Moroccans and their parents in Amsterdam. Labour migrants, such as the Turkish and Moroccan migrants, came with overall low socio-economic and cultural capital. According to segmented assimilation theory, this picture of the parents predicts a downward trajectory in the second generation, with only modest social mobility for the majority of the group and a substantial group that is at risk. However, the actual situation in the second generation is different: The part of both the Turkish and the Moroccan groups that studies in higher education or already has obtained a higher education diploma is larger than the part that leaves school early. The group of early school leavers, about a quarter, is, however, also considerable. If anything, the members of the second generation are characterised by a strong polarisation in their school outcomes. The social mobility patterns among the Turkish and Moroccan Dutch groups show that differences in the conditions under which youngsters go to school have a massive effect on social mobility patterns over time.

Our data further indicate that the young women who attain higher education degrees postpone marriage, choose partners who are also highly educated, and enter the labour market alongside their partners, which further increases the gap with those who are stuck at the bottom of the educational ladder. While assimilation theories put a huge emphasis on ethnic and socio-economic background characteristics of the first generation, our findings show that a lot of the within-group differences result from the dynamics that are rooted in changing attitudes and choices in the second generation itself. The highly-educated second generation propels itself forward with each successive step on their career ladder. Leaving school early as a woman of Turkish or Moroccan descent has a totally different dynamic and results in very different social and socio-economic outcomes. Many do not enter the labour market, they more often marry a partner from the country of migration of their parents, and they more or less reproduce the traditional gender roles in the community. An intersectional approach that includes gender next to ethnicity thus proves helpful here. But it is not only gender, but also age that intersects with social mobility. Belonging to a younger cohort offers more educational opportunities because of the expansion of pre-school facilities or access to help from older siblings with schoolwork and study choices. As a result, the differences within ethnic groups are becoming more pronounced than *between* ethnic groups.

In sum, the heterogeneity of ethnic minority groups is becoming more and more visible. As Glick Schiller and Caglar (2013, 496) point out too, we cannot approach people of the same national or ethnic migrant background homogenously in terms of their values, cultural repertoire, skills, opportunities or identity. This reality demands a new theoretical perspective that sheds more light on the dynamic interplay *between* ethnicity, generation, age cohorts, education, gender, and legal status on the one hand and the majority-minority context of integration in big cities on the other.

The Changed Reality and the Acknowledgement of the Integration Context

The challenges that especially the younger age cohorts face differ from borough to borough within cities as well as between countries. In addition to intersectionality, I thus argue that we additionally need to consider the importance of the integration context.

To illustrate the difference in local challenges, let us look at the city of Amsterdam again. As mentioned, Amsterdam is a majority-minority city. Together, migrants and people with foreign-born parents now make up a little over half of Amsterdam's population. A quarter of the population belongs to the four established migrant groups (from Surinam, the Antilles, Turkey, and Morocco) and the remaining quarter to a large amalgam of migrant groups, which mostly are recent migrants or temporary migrants. We discern differences at the neighbourhood level. In certain parts of the South East district of Amsterdam called the Bijlmer, for instance, people of Dutch descent only form a small minority, around one in five inhabitants at the most (Broekhuizen, van Marissing, & Wonderen, 2012). People of Surinamese descent form the largest group: between a quarter in some and over a third of the residents in other parts. The group of Surinamese descent is itself ethnically very diverse and includes people who originally were brought to Surinam as slaves from Africa, or as "contract" workers from India, China, and Indonesia. Next to the larger groups, about half of the Bijlmer population comes from a myriad of groups among which are people of Moroccan and Turkish descent, new smaller West African groups, and people from the Middle East (Broekhuizen, van Marissing, & Wonderen, 2012). How can this situation be described in terms of integration? Obviously, the children of immigrants in this district do not integrate or assimilate into a Dutch majority group anymore. And though there is a lot of ethnic diversity in the South East district, at the same time there is hardly any socio-economic diversity. We see overall high levels of poverty and a concentration of social housing in high-rise apartment blocks. The neighbourhood also serves as the entry point for many newly-arrived migrants and their families. The schools cater to many children who enter the Dutch school system at a later age and who have little or no command of Dutch.

The Bijlmer is indeed a super-diverse neighbourhood, but of a specific type. The challenges are extensive, but differ from those faced by children of migrants in, say, Amsterdam West and New West. The Amsterdam West and New West neighbourhoods are more socio-economically diverse, and in terms of generations, the inhabitants are more evenly distributed between people of the first, second, and third generations than in the South East district. Here too, people of Dutch descent form a minority, but a larger one than in the Bijlmer. In some neighbourhoods, they make up a third of the population, in others a bit over 40 per cent (Wonderen & Broekhuizen, 2012). In many neighbourhoods in the West and New West district, in the older generation, the group of Dutch descent is still dominant. Children of Dutch descent, together with third generation children of Moroccan and Turkish descent, make up a little over half of the youth population. As such, the super-diverse neighbourhood context in the West yields more positive educational outcomes for children of old and newly-arrived groups (Wonderen &

Broekhuizen, 2012). Research comparing these different types of super-diverse neighbourhoods and different super-diverse situations thus advances our understanding of both super-diversity as a theoretical concept and of differences in integration outcomes.

With regard to differences in social mobility patterns, the polarisation within in the second generation results from a combination of changes in attitudes and practices within communities over time, and changes in the structural conditions in school and neighbourhood contexts. These structural conditions are furthermore country-specific. The national context has a fundamental and defining effect that is drastically altering outcomes. Making use of the integration context theory (Crul & Schneider, 2010), we showed in an earlier publication how institutional arrangements in education and child care shape outcomes in interaction with resources of the first and second generations. Again with the help of the TIES survey, we can look at outcomes for three different national contexts—the Netherlands, Sweden, and Germany. Both Stockholm and Berlin show less polarisation within the second generation than Amsterdam does, but they show opposite outcomes. In Stockholm, the upward social mobility trend is more prominent; while in Berlin the stagnant or downward mobility trend dominates. This immediately shows that, to explain social mobility patterns, we should also take into account the importance of the national integration context.

In Berlin, the overwhelming majority is streamed into vocational education, while in Stockholm, the overwhelming majority is streamed into an academic track. Another remarkable disparity is that, in Berlin, tracking results depend strongly on the educational support of parents, while this is hardly the case in Stockholm (Crul, Schneider, & Lelie, 2012). Different school systems seem to demand different things from parents. Practical support with homework is crucial in the highly stratified system in Germany, while in Stockholm, children work on their homework assignments in school. In Stockholm, pre-school attendance is free of cost and widely available. Second-generation Turkish children are attending pre-school even more often than children of native descent. In Berlin, it is exactly the other way around: Due to higher costs and less availability, many second-generation Turkish children do not attend pre-school at all, or do so only in the last year before entering compulsory education at age five (Crul, Schneider, & Lelie, 2012). This means that parents are largely responsible for teaching their children German as a second language. As a result, many Turkish second generation children start elementary school with a large deficit in the German language. After only four years in elementary school, at age 10, they are already selected into different tracks. It should come as no surprise that so dramatically few children of migrants attend Gymnasium and continue into higher education. At the same time, the drop-out rate is extremely high in Berlin (Crul, Schneider, & Lelie, 2012). In Stockholm, moreover, the female early school leavers and women educated at the middle level almost all participate in the labour market, while in Berlin, the bulk of them do not enter the labour market at all (Crul, Schneider, & Lelie, 2013).

The comparison between the cities demonstrates how various axes of difference interact with contextual factors when explaining different pathways of social mobility. People who are upwardly mobile show a lot of similarities across ethnic groups in terms of pathways and mechanisms. Upward mobility is first characterised by a favourable school context and parents who provide positive educational support. But this only accounts for part of the difference. The gap with the downwardly mobile group is further widened by the change in gender roles that we see in the highly educated group, which results in other choices concerning marriage partners and different decisions about entering the labour market.

The authors of segmented assimilation theory argue that it is the reception in the country of migration and the background characteristics of the first generation that explain differences in social mobility (upward or downward) more than contextual factors. A comparison across local and national integration contexts calls this into question. Our comparison of the cities underscores the necessity of linking the intersection of age, gender, education, and ethnicity to the differences in local institutional arrangements. This, of course, does not mean that between ethnic groups there are no differences in the size of the group that is upwardly or downwardly mobile. Our data illustrates that these differences do not necessarily have an inherently ethnic basis, rather, ethnicity only becomes important in relation to the type of institutional demands made by a particular integration context.

Reflection

Our findings contribute to the general understanding of integration, and of current political and public integration discourses in at least four ways.

First, our thinking about integration in big cities has to change now that there is no longer a majority group in which new groups integrate. Children of new immigrants integrate into neighbourhoods and schools where they primarily interact with other children of immigrants. This makes their integration fundamentally different than previous generations of immigrants.

Second, this also changes the situation for the second and third generation. To still refer to them as "migrants" is not only counterproductive to their process of integration, but also misrepresents reality. In many city districts, these youngsters form the established group receiving newcomers to the city, creating the context for others to adapt to. A considerable group in the second generation holds professional positions in which they actually shape the opportunities for others in the cities rather than being on the receiving end of the process.

Third, next to what new migrants can do themselves to become successful in school or the labour market given their own resources and their drive to succeed, the influence of the integration context is often overlooked. Differences in opportunities school systems offer in terms of pre-school, late selection, and apprenticeships are crucial for their successful integration.

Fourth, and high on the political agenda nowadays, is the emancipation of young immigrant women. Findings show that their emancipation is the result of educational success and not of the popular demand for assimilation of migrants and their children in dominant national culture and values. Gender roles change dramatically in a context providing good opportunities for girls to be successful in school. In a negative school environment with few opportunities for girls to be academically successful, gender roles hardly change.

How do we develop new policies for super-diverse cities, neighbourhoods, and schools? Policies that are more adjusted to the rapidly changing realities in our cities? Diversity will be the new norm in super-diverse cities. This calls for a paradigmatic shift. After decades of programs targeting immigrants and children, we need to switch our thinking completely. The group that is most adapted to the new city reality are the children and grandchildren of immigrants that have been born and have grown up in the city. For instance, they have the most ethnically diverse friendship groups. The young people of Dutch decent are most closed up in their own ethnic group; they are the least adapted to the new demographic reality of the city. The highly educated second generation can in many ways be especially seen as leading the way to the future. This is visible, for instance, in the arts where there is an expansion in creativity by young second and third generation artists in literature, theatre, as stand-up comedians, film and documentary makers, journalists, and columnists. Any new policy that embraces the new reality in the city should start with this group. They are the group most adjusted to the new super-diverse reality of our cities. They can lead the way in so-far uncharted terrain. With two-thirds of children under the age of fifteen being (grand)children of immigrants in Amsterdam, it is clear who will inherit the city—economically, socially, and culturally. Institutions will either need to accept that new reality or they will slowly wither away.

---

[1] *This article presents a summary of the findings and insights of our TIES survey, which have been previously published in Crul (2015) and Crul, Schneider & Lelie (2012, 2013).*

References

Alba, R., Jimenéz, T., & Marrow, H. (2009). Mexican Americans as a paradigm for contemporary intra-group heterogeneity. *Ethnic and Racial Studies*, 37(3), 446–466.

Alba, R., & Nee, V. (2003). R*emaking the American mainstream: Assimilation and contemporary immigration.* Cambridge, MA: Harvard University Press.

Blommaert, J., & Maly, I. (2014). Inleiding. Superdiversiteit, introductie van een nieuw paradigma. In I. Maly, J. Blommaert, & J. Ben Yakoub (Eds.), *Superdiversiteit en Democratie.* Brussels: Epo.

Broekhuizen, J., van Marissing, E., & Wonderen, R. (2012). *Samenleven met verschillen in Zuidoost.* Amsterdam: Verwey Jonker Intsituut & Bureau Onderzoek en Statistiek.

Crul, M. (2015). Super-diversity vs. assimilation: how complex diversity in majority–minority cities challenges the assumptions of assimilation. In: *Journal of Ethnic and Migration Studies*, DOI: 10.1080/1369183X.2015.1061425

Crul, M., & Schneider, J. (2010). Comparative integration context theory: Participation and belonging in new diverse European cities. *Ethnic and Racial Studies*, 33(7), 1249–1268.

Crul, M., Schneider, J., & Lelie, F. (2012). The European second generation compared: *Does the integration context matter?* Amsterdam: Amsterdam University Press.

Crul, M., Schneider, J., & Lelie, F. (2013). Super-diversity: *A new perspective on integration.* Amsterdam: VU University Press.

Glick Schiller, N., & Caglar, A. (2013). Locating migrant pathways of economic emplacement: Thinking beyond the ethnic lens. *Ethnicities*, 13(4), 494–514.

Meissner, F. (2015). Migration in migration-related diversity? The nexus between superdiversity and migration studies. E*thnic and Racial Studies,* 38(4), 556–567.

Meissner, F., & Vertovec, S. (2015). Comparing superdiversity. **Ethnic and Racial Studies,** 38, 541–555.

Portes, A., & Rumbaut, R. (2001). Legacies: *The story of the immigrant second generation.* Los Angeles: University of California Press.

Portes, A., & Zhou, M. (1993). The new second generation: Segmented assimilation and its variants. *Annals*, 530, 74–96.

Vertovec, S. (2007). Super-diversity and its implications. *Ethnic and Racial Studies*, 30(6), 1024–1054.

Waters, M. C., Tran, V., Kasinitz, P., & Mollenkopf, J. (2010). Segmented assimilation revisited: Types of acculturation and socioeconomic mobility in young adulthood. E*thnic and Racial Studies*, 33(7), 1168–1193.

Wonderen, R., & Broekhuizen, J. (2012). *Samenleven met verschillen in Nieuw West.* Amsterdam: Verwey Jonker Intsituut & Bureau Onderzoek en Statistiek (O+S).

Musicians
Music Generations

10. Challenging Social Cohesion and Citizenship

Sandra Trienekens

Look at the world around us: it is on fire. Look at the strong anti-Islamic attitude among a large part of the population in the Western world; look at the Islamic terrorists and what ISIS is doing in the Middle East. And then, when I watch our MusicGenerations group sing peacefully together, all of a sudden, I feel deeply touched. Apparently, it is not as difficult as the politicians make us believe, to bring people together and have them collaborate regardless of background and religion. Moreover, I have gotten to an age where many of my friends and acquaintances would rather stay home than go out. I am increasingly left to my own devices to go and find new activities so that I can continue to enjoy a night out. And when and where can we old people really engage with the younger generation? We hardly ever actively meet. Therefore, it is great to work with all these people—young and old—at MusicGenerations. Even if the young guys are a little loud at times during rehearsals, I don't mind—coming here gives me energy. (Interview with older female singer)

Political and public obsession with social cohesion can be considered a typically western phenomenon. Many highly diverse societies, in the Caribbean for instance, are not familiar with social cohesion policies. But the issue of social cohesion has kept Dutch society in its grip for quite some time now. One thing everyone seems to agree on is that a society never has enough of it. Also these days, consensus is growing among Dutch politicians, academics, journalists, and so on, that our society lacks social cohesion and that there was more of it in the past (SCP, 2008). Although the precise definition of social cohesion remains unspecified, there is also, by and large, consensus on the source of the problem: the process of individualisation and migration. According to the common belief, people show less solidarity nowadays, they do not greet one another or help one another out anymore. Additionally, the allegedly strong internal cohesion within ethnic groups is thought to hamper migrants' identification within society at large. One collectively wonders what is going to hold our highly differentiated, polarised societies together.

This chapter explores the premises on which this problem definition of social cohesion is based. One such premise is that social cohesion must manifest itself on the national level, can be complete and needs to be "thick," i.e., measured—as is often done by Dutch statisticians—by the number of inter-ethnic relationships. In spite of actual developments toward and postmodernist conceptions of fluid borders and global communities, when it comes to integration of migrants, the national context continues to frame our thinking. This stands in the way of a more "realistic" analysis of the current "level of cohesion" in society, which will consequently always be partial and the relationships people build with the national state will differ according to their transnational and/or global affiliations. This is, however, no threat to society's macro stability. There is research pointing out the strength of weak ties, such as Granovetter's back in the early 1970s, overthrowing the idea of a need for "thick cohesion."

Another premise expresses itself in the dominance of ethnicity and religion as indicators in political, public, and academic analyses of the "problems" of contemporary society. Ethnicity and religion are interpreted as primary markers of identity. This cultural thinking, in which the notion of a "national culture" is also still upheld, continues to divide the "Moroccans" or the "Turks" from the "Dutch," even when the people referred to were all born and raised in the Netherlands. Ghorashi (2010) concludes that two assumptions in the Dutch history of migration have not changed since the 1970s. The first assumption is that migrants constitute a separate, non-compatible group in society. She labels this assumption the "culturalisation tendency" (2010, p. 13) and here she discerns a relationship to the former organisation of Dutch society in Protestant, Catholic, and Humanist communities living alongside one another, tolerating but not engaging with one another. The second is a "deficit assumption" referring to the persistent perception of migrants as "less developed," and, thus, in need of help (to be offered by welfare state organisations) to catch up with the modern state of affairs in the host society. On the basis of a meta-analysis of academic publications on social cohesion, Harell and Stolle (2011) come to a similar conclusion. They show that the way in which the social sciences have defined social cohesion in the past 20 years or so take one or all of the following features as a requirement for a "shared community": shared identity, (national) cultural homogeneity, and value consensus. In such conceptualisations, Harell and Stolle maintain, diversity, i.e., the presence of people with different ethnicities and religions among the population, and social cohesion cannot be satisfactorily reconciled. Add the assumptions Ghorashi discerned, and "smooth" integration or "healthy" social cohesion are indeed hard to envision. If Dutch society indeed suffers from a problem with social cohesion, it is to a large extent self-inflicted.

The practice of MusicGenerations shows us several alternative images, "small realities," that dismantle such premises. As such, it inspires future-oriented conceptions of society's diversity, integration, and social cohesion. For instance, although culture (both in the anthropological and the artistic meaning of the word) can be a dividing force, MusicGenerations shows the way in which culture (music) can have a binding quality. Moreover, it gives insight into "society's state of total diversity," in which even people from the former white majority no longer apply a one-dimensional frame of (national) cultural reference. In such a context, the demand for the assimilation of migrants into "Dutch national culture" is unrealistic, if not: absurd. MusicGenerations shows that the problem of segregation may be smaller than commonly perceived, and above all, that the "gap" seems to be easily closed when people are approached in the right manner. MusicGenerations allows us to perceive people as individuals, rather than as group members. One quickly becomes aware that there is more to people's identity than merely their ethnicity or religion. MusicGenerations shows that the fact that we are all different does not stand in the way of collaboration. In a sufficiently mixed group, "difference" becomes quotidian and values other than those related to ethnic cultures or religions begin to function as binding forces. Additionally, it becomes clear that more people than our right-wing politicians would have us believe share "western values." Finally, MusicGenerations gives us an indication of what may constitute social bonds and citizenship in our contemporary and future society. A relational and non-emotional approach could help us to move beyond the alleged necessity of shared cultures and values and homogenous cultural identities, which have supported concepts such as social cohesion and citizenship for the longest time, but have done little other than reinforce cultural differences.

The insights presented in this chapter are based on research on the MusicGenerations "Talent for Freedom" programme, conducted in the first half of 2015. By drawing from the observations, interviews, and questionnaire, I explore the restructuring power of MusicGenerations' "small realities," i.e., pockets of reality that exists alongside the reality of the dominant narratives in society. As such, MusicGenerations is treated here as an example of how society could function if we wanted it to.

How Bad is the State of Social Cohesion in our Society?

Even if the term "social cohesion" is not always explicitly used, policy papers and/or programmes continue to be directed at fighting polarisation or at facilitating encounters between people from a myriad of backgrounds. But how bad is the state of social cohesion in our society? Pretty bad if "absolute cohesion," whatever that may be, is the ultimate goal. As mentioned, social cohesion will always be partial. It will never encompass everyone and certainly not with the same intensity or strength, because people will develop different kinds of relationships with society. There will also always be extremist parties that withdraw from the general society. Moreover, when we direct our analysis to the local level, we have to conclude that, generally speaking, society is doing relatively well in cohesive terms. There are no daily reports of fights between people of different ethnic backgrounds in our highly diverse urban boroughs. Many workplaces are diverse in terms of the employees' ethnic backgrounds and so are schools. Research shows the existence of super-diverse networks at the local level (Blommaert, 2013). Additionally, if we would cease to label young Dutch people as "second, third, and fourth generation Surinamese, Moroccan, or Turkish migrants," the need for analyses of inter-ethnic friendships would be much more difficult to defend. Polemical as it may be, the point I am trying to make is that the picture of the cohesive state of our society is distorted by the way in which we categorise our citizens into ethnic groups and that the actual state may not be as bad as commonly perceived.

Nonetheless, social cohesion has become part of our vocabulary and pops up—almost matter-of-factly—in problem definitions in many a policy document. A second point I would like to make is that we should be more careful and precise in formulating what the problem is. The problem may be political or socio-economical in nature, rather than having to do primarily with social cohesion. For instance, one is concerned about the strong, even at times extreme reaction to the accommodation of refugees in several (small) Dutch villages. The first question needs to be why this is the case? Are the refugees the problem, or is it something else? Such as the authorities that lose track of proportions: wanting to accommodate 1,400 refugees in a village of around 150 inhabitants (rtvdrenthe.nl 2016). Or is the socio-economic precariousness of the people who protest the actual problem? Or did the people act out of ignorance (lack of contact with migrants and their descendants), or are they indeed racist? Heijne maintains that people's reactions are often extreme because of the strong discontent they feel, and have for a long time: "Many people feel that they are being overlooked, that others—in the name of humanistic and humanitarian principles—count for more than they do, that only their wallets are interesting, that the pillars of their world—culture, community, small scale—are being taken from them in the name of abstract, lofty principles" (Heijne, 2012, p. 13; Heijne, 2016). In such instances, the solution is not the instigation of a policy or funding programme on social cohesion. If the problem is indeed a matter of cohesion, we should be explicit about which ties need to be strengthened. The message should be that there is no problem with the overall cohesion in our society, just between specific groups. E.g., that particularly the former white majority nurtures highly homogeneous networks (see chapter 9).

MusicGenerations teaches us a lesson in this regard. Groot carefully selects the boroughs she works in and the people she works with. She is aware that, in diverse urban boroughs, strong local networks exist and that, in general terms, there is no issue with social cohesion. Nonetheless, she is aware that, in these boroughs, it is white seniors and youngsters, i.e., a colourful group of people, who can make life difficult for one another. That has become one of the rationales for working intergenerationally in super-diverse urban settings. Moreover, Groot travelled with music director Paul Mayer and several MusicGenerations talents to Oranje, the village of 150 people mentioned above, shortly after the incidents, to celebrate a musical Christmas with joint concerts by the villagers and the refugees (dvhn.nl 2015). Because, whereas politicians caused the problem, Groot realised that it would still be good to clear the air and bring the parties involved together in a positive, even reconciliatory manner.

Society's Total State of Diversity

MusicGenerations' bringing together of people from different ethnic and socio-economic backgrounds, ages, and cultural preferences supersedes the common "ethnic" interpretation of diversity. By bringing in age in an intergenerational constellation, as well as responding to shared passions that allow for both sharing and differing, MusicGenerations shows us that diversity is about all these things: ethnicity, age, cultural taste, and so on. "Super-diversity" is the concept with which scholars currently attempt to capture the complex interplay of the different indicators of identity. It is the concept that MusicGenerations has come to adopt in the course of its development.

While scholars may still be debating whether the present day complexity and social differences are larger than in earlier periods in history (cf. Lucassen & Penninx, 1997), the popular representations and political discourses of recent years are evidently dominated by "diversity talk." Vertovec—who coined the term "super-diversity"—maintains that we are living "in the age of diversity" (2012, p. 287). When Vertovec first developed the notion of super-diversity (2007), he did so to capture the changing dynamics of Britain's urban landscape and it has since been used to characterize contemporary modern societies more generally. He proposed the thesis that changing social and political configurations since the early 1990s resulted in the "diversification of diversity." While pre-1990 and post-World War II migration to Europe stemmed from a limited number of countries and the group of migrants ("guest workers") was rather homogenous in terms of socioeconomic, cultural, and religious backgrounds (cf. Parkin and Arnaut, 2012), post-1990 migration is characterised by smaller numbers of migrants from many places and by a high degree of variation in gender, human capital, age, space, migration channels, as well as legal statuses.

With super-diversity Vertovec (2007, p. 1024) thus drew our attention to the dynamic interplay of variables among the new, small and scattered, multiple-origin, transnationally connected, socio-economically differentiated, and legally stratified immigrants who have arrived in Europe since the 1990s. Vertovec called (2007, p. 1025) for a reshaping and extension of existing frameworks that solely or predominantly focus on ethnicity, to consider multiple axes of differentiation. Meissner (2014, pp. 1-5), among others, argues accordingly that super-diversity can be seen as: a) a set of variables that researchers conjunctively investigate, and b) as a context in which different variables play out in complex patterns. This means that anyone adopting a super-diversity lens would attempt to capture both the specificity of different super-diverse contexts, and how multiple variables are simultaneously at play in these contexts, influencing various actors, institutions, and localities differently.

Even though widely used and celebrated, the concept of super-diversity does not come without limitations. First and foremost, it is a concept that above all expresses blindness on the side of white scholars. For any migrant, in any historical period, it is apparent that migrants are not a homogenous group. Given this blindness, evidently, a concept such as super-diversity is needed to drive the message home to the (white) dominant segment of society; the part that dominates our governments, boards, academia, and other positions of power.

Super-diversity thus suffers from an (im)migration focus. As Anthias (2012, p. 105) aptly puts it: "Diversity in society exists at multiple levels and not only in terms of minority ethnic or migrant groups, and therefore the recognition of differentiated and complex migrant statuses and locations is only one facet of social diversity." Whereas super-diversity initially served as a call to move beyond the mere focus on ethnicity, it should perhaps be moved more explicitly beyond the sole focus on non-western migrants and come to acknowledge more thoroughly the super-diversity among western migrants and even among the former majority as well.

"There are scholars who more explicitly integrate the former majority into their description of the diversification of diversity."

There are scholars who more explicitly integrate the former majority into their description of the diversification of diversity (e.g. Blommaert, 2013; Prins, 2013). Blommaert indeed points toward the changes in migration patterns since the 1990s. But he also discerns a multi-layered ethnic composition of migrant neighbourhoods in western cities and the emergence of diverse networks around housing, labour, and sometimes even religion, e.g., mixed churches. Also the "white" middle-class, buying property in these areas, is tied into these networks. A second development he incorporates into his analysis is the widespread availability of new technology since the early 1990s. This has led to the emergence of global networks in terms of finance, trade, and power, but also in the everyday lives of ordinary people. One aspect of this second development is the emergence of global social networks. These networks are not deprived of culture, but it is a "democratic culture" rather than an ethnic or national culture that binds them together. Buck-Morss (2014) refers to these with the term "global crowd": a force that self-organizes through social media and does not need leaders (cf. "Empire" by Hardt & Negri, 2000). Another aspect, I would like to add, is the fact that transnationality can be considered a trait of many families of the former majority as well. Either one or more children live abroad, or the children live in the Netherlands but with a foreign partner. I conducted a (very) quick scan of the composition of two regular primary school classes, one in Amsterdam-West and the other in Amsterdam-South, i.e., two relatively "white" neighbourhoods, to illustrate this point. The quick scan revealed that each class contains less than a handful of children with two parents from an entirely Dutch genealogy. The other "white" children are from bi-national families, for instance, Dutch-Argentinian, Dutch-Portuguese, Dutch-German, Dutch-Finnish, or from tri-national families, with for instance, one Indonesian-Dutch and one Canadian parent, or the children are from expat families (Western but non-Dutch).

Taking these large-scale developments together, Blommaert concludes that western societies have fundamentally changed. These societies are now characterised by the mobility of all its citizens, whether former migrants or former majority. Another characteristic is fragmentation, since former static categories have become fluid and alliances change rapidly. This means that stability is no longer a social given. These characteristics describe our societies, individual urban neighbourhoods, and the lives of individual citizens. Together, they define our "super-diverse" society, according to Blommaert.

I propose we use the superlative of "super-diversity" and refer to this phenomenon as "society's" state of total diversity. This to further stress the point that we need to relieve the emphasis on the "ethnic." Because when the number of (urban) residents with a one-dimensional Dutch cultural frame of reference is also diminishing among the former majority, the alleged "bearers of the Dutch national culture and identity," the call for assimilation of migrants and their children in the "former majority culture" becomes even more abstruse. If all our identities and everyday lives are characterised by total diversity, if we are all different, then no one really is. If there is no longer a clear ethnic and cultural majority, then, as Crul and colleagues (2013, p. 14) also argue, everyone has to adjust and adapt.

MusicGenerations does not only present us a group of people who are diverse in terms of age, socio-economic backgrounds, life experiences, musical tastes, and lifestyles. "Talent for Freedom" shows that mixing is already a reality.

The concerts make us aware not only of the Turkish-Dutch girl being fond of Dutch chansons or the Kurdish-Dutch girl who just wants to sing professionally (and not only Kurdish songs). They also draw our attention to the Dutch-Dutch girl touring Europe singing in Zazaki, one of the Kurdish languages, that she has familiarised herself with and has come to love so much through MusicGenerations.

Doing Away with Age Segregation

Hagestad and Uhlenberg (2006) provide a history of how social scientists have viewed age as both an integrative and a segregative force in society. They point toward age's complex links to the division of labour, but elaborate on the relation of age to social integration. They maintain that, for older adults, ties to children and grandchildren represent possibilities for learning and the development of generativity: investment in the lives of others and in the future of human communities. The link between cross-generational ties and generativity appears to be particularly clear for men. The authors consider the family more or less to be the only surviving age-integrated institution. The authors wonder if we can rely on families to counter the potentially negative consequences of societal age segregation. They see other domains in contemporary Western societies as marked by widespread institutional, spatial, and cultural age segregation.

In governmental programmes and the academic literature, one also encounters a fear for (further) separation between the generations, the ensuing unrealistic and negative stereotypes between them, and a consequent decrease in positive encounters. For instance, this is stated as the reason why the European Commission (EC) encourages its member states to build intergenerational networks. The EC promotes intergenerational learning as part of Lifelong Learning: generations working together to gain skills, values, and knowledge. The aim is social cohesion as well as community building. With regard to community building, the EC points out that the generations have resources of value to each other and share areas of concern. For example, both the younger and older generations are often marginalised in decision-making that directly affects their lives. The EC understands intergenerational learning as an effective way to address key government priorities, such as building active communities, promoting citizenship, regenerating neighbourhoods, and addressing inequality.

The practice of MusicGenerations nuances the fear for further segregation to some extent.

The practice of MusicGenerations nuances the fear for further segregation to some extent. It shows that many participants are part of intergenerational constellations due to family and/or work ties (cf. Gowricharn, 2015, p. 10). Moreover, the practice of MusicGenerations shows that the participants really enjoy collaborating. It is hard to trace the origin of the idea that old and young people would not like to work together or spend time together. MusicGenerations illustrates that they do:

The collaboration brings the different generations joy. The participants greet one another with a hug, they enjoy each other's company, and they happily sing duets together. There may be disagreements at times, as in any participatory project, but openness and spontaneity prevail. (Observations)

The participants actively seek out intergenerationality. The two main reasons to participate, mentioned by the participants, are "I just like singing" and "I like singing together with people from many different backgrounds and ages." (Questionnaire)

The older Dutch-Dutch participants especially tell me that they experience a lack of interaction with the younger generation in their daily lives. For them, MusicGenerations is indeed an intergenerational meeting place. (Interviews)

Also, with regard to how the generations meet in a constructive way, we can learn from MusicGenerations. Because even more than a lack of contact, there seems to be a lack of space where the generations can build non-hierarchical relationships:

One of the participants, a secondary school gymnastics teacher, tells me: "Even though I work with youngsters, MusicGenerations has been both a great and new experience. Where else do you experience such great enthusiasm in young people when they see you, even go out of their way to come up to you to greet and hug you? And we all sing together; an 80-year-old sings a duet with a 16-year-old. Tell me, what is there not to like?! Interaction with the young people at work is quite different—more hierarchical. In MusicGenerations, there is never a situation of 'us' and 'them.' No one is telling others what to do. There is no need to discuss age diversity with the young people. Both sides enjoy it—that is enough!" (Interview with a Dutch-Dutch older female singer)

Furthermore, there seems to be a lack of encounters in which the generations meet as *equally talented people*—as opposed to encounters around the "exchange of resources" such as the EC suggests. Although one may certainly learn to respect the other for knowledge or experience one does not possess oneself. The unity, mutual support, and collective fun which the stage image of "Talent for Freedom" conveys (see chapter 4), seems to suggest, however, that working from equal talents, shared passions, and non-hierarchical relationships results in a more thorough identification and connection with "the other."

Doing Away with Persistent Group-Thinking

Research on post-World War II migration has been dominated by the focus on *community* (cf. Flint & Robinson, 2008). Explanations were primarily based on the (culture of the) migrants' country of origin and other group-based attributes, although there may have been a scholarly shift from group-based attributes to more individual characteristics, which parallels broader shifts toward individualization and cosmopolitanisation (cf. Beck, 2011), Ghorashi (2010) shows that, for the Netherlands, policy and political discourse on integration did not follow suit. Migrants and their (grand)children continue to be perceived of as separate groups in society.

Several scholars have by now pointed toward the dynamics in cultural identities, Doucerain and colleagues, among others (2013). Frustrated by the limits of the bidimensional approach in (statistical) acculturation research, they developed a survey tool that would do better justice to the lived experiences of migrants and their descendants in the multicultural context of Canada. Their tool offered respondents space to list the cultural groups they identify with. In addition to "mainstream," e.g., English-Canadian, French-Canadian, and "heritage," e.g., Chinese, Haitian groups—with the possibility of selecting more than one group per category—participants were also encouraged to include "hybrid" cultural groups, e.g., Chinese-Canadian, religious or spiritual affiliations, and other salient cultural identities. The participants were then asked to reconstruct their activities of the previous day and to indicate the people and language(s) involved in the activities. This showed that participants switched cultural affiliations several times during the day. This finding underscores the fluid nature of acculturation, i.e., integration. Doucerain and colleagues (2013, p. 697) maintain that better insight into how micro-variation and macro-stability can well go hand in hand, can potentially broaden our understanding of the concept of "integration" to an understanding of individuals' fluidly shifting cultural identification and cultural frames of reference. Such a fluid understanding radically differs from more static notions of biculturalism or hybridity suggesting, at most, a bicultural frame switching.

Logical and understandable as these dynamic cultural affiliations are, they have not yet penetrated the commonplace perceptions of our professionals nor the daily routines and procedures that support our society's functioning. Nonetheless, scholars working on intersectionality have already made this point extensively. Intersectionality originated in race and gender studies (e.g. Anthias & Yuval Davis, 1983, 1992; Anthias, 1992; Brah, 1992; Wekker, 1992) and stresses the importance of looking at how multiple social processes and structures intertwine to produce specific social positions and identities (Anthias, 2012, p. 106). It implies that one has to simultaneously take into account categories such as ethnicity, gender, and class in order to grasp the multifaceted nature of our social world and explain positions of advantage and disadvantage therein. The key point is that each division intersects with the others (cf. Collins, 1993; Crenshaw, 1994); people are always more than just one element of their identity. Thus, identity and ethnicity should not be conflated. Which element of their identity people like to emphasise depends on the situation they are in. From this multi-layered identities approach, Essed (2001, p. 504) and Solomos (2001) built a dynamic and political approach to identity. They emphasise that identity formation takes shape in dynamic interaction with dominant and counter-ideologies and social discourses, norms, and values. However, identity-formation is a two-way process. One has to figure out who one wants to be and what one's place in society might be. In turn, society needs to give one space to do so.

The case of "Talent for Freedom" shows us that, rather than treating migrants and their descendants as group members with group identities, one better zooms in on the identity construction of individuals:

Self-definition is at the heart of the practice of MusicGenerations. The first questions new talents are being asked are: "Who are you?" "What is your talent?" and "What would you like to do in 'Talent for Freedom?" The talents can be heard saying things like "I'm from Indonesia, but I'd rather sing jazz" or "I'm retired and I like to rap." Ethnicity and age both appear to be weak predictors of taste and cultural preference. (Observations)

When asked if she feels recognised by MusicGenerations' choice of songs, a Turkish-Dutch girl answers: "I feel partly recognised. Unfortunately no Turkish songs are part of the repertoire. Nonetheless, there are several Dutch songs that I really love singing and listening to." (Interview)

Other participants answer that they do not adhere to just one specific cultural tradition. One of them maintains: "The focus of the programme is on freedom rather than on cultural traditions and that is the way it should be!" (Questionnaire)

Hence, the answers provided by the participants teach us a lesson about identity; they show that identities are both complex and non-static. Identities can be built on several cultural traditions simultaneously. Sometimes one emphasizes an ethnic-cultural trait of one's identity; at other times one presents oneself first and foremost as, e.g., a singer or vocalist. Or, in other words, "we need to be aware that people move into and out of contexts of diversity and operate in multiple layers of identification" (Arnaut, 2012, p. 4):

The nonlinearity between ethnicity and (cultural) identity—and the part of one's identity one would like to show on stage—is expressed in the combination of participants and songs. Three older men sing a Dutch version of the Beastie Boys' song "Fight for Your Right (to Party)," meaning: old does not equal "lack of vitality" and everyone should be free to decide who they want to be and how they want to live. (Observations)

Another example is the duet of the Kurdish song "Venge Yeno" by a Kurdish-Dutch and a Dutch-Dutch girl. This song was part of the MusicGenerations repertoire before there ever were any participants with Kurdish roots. The Kurdish-Dutch girl who recently joined MusicGenerations was pleasantly surprised when she learned about the repertoire and felt welcome as a consequence. Up until now, she mainly sang within the safe circle of the Alevi community she participates in. She enjoys singing and sharing this song— about repression and fleeing from their territory—with others outside her community. She says: "This way the song can trigger other emotions and reactions than the usual ones in our community. But above all, I want to sing—in whatever language—with the support of professional musicians and music directors, and I want to perform on stage." (Interview)

Conversely, the Dutch-Dutch girl, who never had anything to do with Kurdistan or its cultural tradition, fell in love with the Kurdish language and music when she joined MusicGenerations. In earlier editions of the programme, she came in contact with Kurdish songs, began learning the Zazaki language and has since been performing in this language at concerts in several European countries. (Interview)

> The ability to develop one's own identity and cultural affiliations is one of the interpretations of freedom one encounters in the practice of MusicGenerations

The ability to develop one's own identity and cultural affiliations is one of the interpretations of freedom one encounters in the practice of MusicGenerations. Often, a tension exists between self-definition and recognition by one's family or cultural community and one between reductionism and cultural sensitivity by society at large. In everyday life, as Ghorashi explains (2010, p. 1), individuals expect fellow citizens to recognise their cultural background, but they don't want their fellow citizens to reduce them to bearers of a static, monolithic culture. Here too, it is a two-way street. One has to figure out who one wants to be and what one's place in society might be. In turn, society needs to give one space to do so. The personal struggles for freedom, such as those several of the young MusicGenerations talents alluded to, indicate that the expectations of both their families and of the wider society are still strongly connected to the etnocultural roots. Only when the wider society begins to accept all young people born in the Netherlands as Dutch (also when their grandparents were migrants), can they begin feeling that they belong in the Netherlands and bloom in the full complexity of their identity.

Doing Away with Non-Compatibility

We can still discern an "us-them" thinking. The alleged incompatibility is manifest in the juxtaposition of oriental and occidental traditions and values, in political and public debates. This refers to a "deficit assumption," the second constant that Ghorashi (2010) discerned in the Dutch history of migration. Specifically, non-western (Muslim) migrants are being depicted as a threat to Western values such as freedom of speech, democracy, self-determination, equality between races and sexes, as Lucassen (2005) has shown. Consequently, populist right-wing politicians promote themselves as defenders of western norms and values (including homosexuality) against conservative religious Islamists. But how western are these values? On the one hand, Lucassen (2005, p. 3) rightly points out a curious amnesia about the deeply rooted anti-Semitism in Western Europe, at least until World War II. The UN-Committee on the Elimination of Racial Discrimination (CERD, 2015; cf. Essed, 1991) established that the Dutch government invests too little in the prevention of discrimination in almost all societal domains the Committee looked into. Moreover, do contemporary European extremist factions—both nationalist and religious—not ignore these values to a large extent too? On the other hand, are liberation movements and freedom fighters across the globe—from Arab, Asian, and Latin-American countries—not fighting to achieve precisely these values, to free themselves from repressive, conservative (religious) regimes? And are these destructive regimes not often helped to power by Western forces, due to an oversimplification by Western political leaders of the complex reality they are facing both at home and in the countries where they intervene, such as Afghanistan and Iraq, as e.g., Adam Curtis' documentary "Bitter Lake" blatantly shows?

The American historian Buck-Morss sets out to unravel the misconception of the existence of clearly distinguishable civilizations—a Eurocentric notion prevalent among historians and political scientists, captured and elaborated in Samuel Huntington's 1996 best-selling book *The Clash of Civilizations and the Remaking of World Order*. Buck-Morss illustrates interrelations and intertwining events throughout the shared history of East and West, and maintains that if human invention does not take place in a vacuum, its products cannot belong to any part of humanity exclusively. "Hence, across slices of time, the giant social units called civilization are spaces so ecumenically shared that they are not one collective's restricted inheritance" (Buck-Morss, 2014, p. 83).

She continues to dismantle the related idea of certain parts of the world being more civilized or democratic than others. With reference to *horizontalidad* in Argentina's protests during the economic crisis of 2001-2002, the Arab Spring, the World Social Forum and Occupy movements, she points out that these democratic successes happened without paternal leaders, without foreign teachers, without invading armies. Meaning:

It was not a case of Egyptians or Tunisians catching up with the West. Rather, they were showing the rest of the world the way. (...) The global movements now happening in the name of democracy bear witness to the fact that democracy is an unfinished project not because it has yet to spread sufficiently in the world but, rather, because democracy as conceived within Western modernity has been insufficient (indeed, deficient) from the start. (Buck-Morss, 2014, p. 86)

In the previous chapter, Crul showed that the Western context has strong influence on how conservative or progressive the "second generation" is. Progressive values, such as equality between men and women, are embraced as a consequence of social-economic upward mobility, which in turn is triggered by an educational system that is supportive of non-native speakers, by good childcare facilities and access to the labour market for these young Dutch people. Özdil (2015, p. 52) brings to our attention that, if the Dutch government had not gone down the path of "integrating migrants whilst maintaining their cultural identity" in the 1980s—which factually meant public financial support of ultraconservative, right-wing, nationalistic organisations from the countries of origin— that the first generation migrants' outlook at the world would be radically different today.

The practice of MusicGenerations points in a similar direction. The set list of the "Talent for Freedom" concerts contains songs that refer to different fights for freedom in many parts of the world, bringing to mind the history of slavery and World War II as well as present day oppression, ethnic cleansing, and expulsion of ethnic or religious minorities from their lands. As the diverse group of vocal talents stands united on stage, they take a clear collective stance: our current freedom is a luxury, we need to defend it together. It is the older participants who have had the experience in Japanese internment camps or with World War II in Europe. The Surinamese-Dutch and Antillean-Dutch participants are particularly aware of the history of slavery. But the young participants are well aware of the importance of freedom in general and several of them tell me about their struggles for personal freedom growing up in the Netherlands and their emancipation from both their parents' and the dominant culture.

The MusicGenerations' talents thus not only share a passion for music. For them, freedom is also a shared value. With regard to working from shared values, two statements can be made. First, working from shared passions and values is a powerful way to connect people and open up dialogue in which there is room for recognition and differing. Over the last fifteen years, MusicGenerations' programmes have shown that shared passions (love of music), shared values ("the act of believing"), and the jointly felt urgency to defend our freedom, are able to communicate similarities and communalities.

Moreover, the differences in experience or interpretation of these values do not disappear in the programmes, but neither do they stand in the way of dialogue, of collaborating, of having fun together. It shows us that "diversity" or "difference" is not necessarily a dividing factor. Second, MusicGenerations sheds a different light on alleged insurmountable differences. Even religious musical leaders could reach agreement; "Turks" and "Kurds" stand hand in hand on stage.

My intention is not to deny the existence of conservative, religious forces, destructive to democratic developments and hampering people's freedom in Muslim countries or among Muslims living in the West. The point is that conservatism, or "backwardness" as right-wing politicians like to call it, is not a "natural," in-born characteristic of certain nations or peoples. Nor is it my intention to defend notions such as that everyone ultimately is a "good person." But even if people are primarily fighters, egoists, aimed at conquering the other, again, some are not more so than others. Societies will need to correct citizens' lack of democracy or their hampering of other people's freedom. But these societies will have to be introspective too and admit to their own exclusionary practices.

Reasons for Contact and Encounters

There appears to be strong consensus among politicians, social professionals and scholars about the importance of having people from different backgrounds meet. Time and again, scholars from various academic disciplines have proven the necessity for the meeting of and contact between societal groups. As early as 1954, Allport stressed in his contact theory that contact between groups can effectively reduce negative attitudes toward out-groups. More recently, studies by, e.g., Hewstone et al. (2007), Savelkou et al. (2011), and Crul et al. (2013) have provided comparable insights.

Wessendorf (2013) nuances, however, that public and associational encounters do not necessarily lead to a deeper intercultural understanding. Wessendorf, among others, shows that, while people may mix in terms of cultural differences in public as well as associational spaces, this rarely translates to private relationships. Gidley summarises: "Public interculturalism is often accompanied by private segregation" (2013, p. 367). Also, commonplace diversity does not necessarily mean the absence of tension and racism. Shared practices and living together in diverse localities does not preclude conflict, as "people are capable of acting in both cosmopolitan and racist ways at different moments, in different contexts" (Noble, 2011, p. 158). Moreover, societies become increasingly divided between citizens who are willing to help with the accommodation of newly arriving migrants and those who fear the arrival of these very people. In other words, between those who believe in "Wir schaffen das" and those who believe in building "fortresses" by closing national (if not European) borders. Nonetheless, prejudice can be heightened in the absence of such encounters, according to Wessendorf, who also stresses the importance of providing opportunities for contact both in terms of shaping attitudes toward one another more generally as well as enabling people "to change their views over time and thus reduce entrenched views about others" (2010, p. 409). In this regard, Padilla and colleagues (2014, p. 12; cf. Ghorashi, 2010, p. 131) show that in spaces, characterized by heterogeneity, "difference" or "otherness" is internalized and may become a quotidian positive feature. Hence, there exists a clear need for facilitating platforms for exchange and contact so that relationships can be built between people from all walks of life. The practice of MusicGenerations underscores such findings and shows that the arts can function as a platform for interaction and exchange (cf. Trienekens & Hillaert, 2015). Creating such a platform is indeed the rationale behind the MusicGenerations programme.

The participants told me that they knew about other generations or cultures, but did not always know people with different backgrounds personally before. One Dutch-Dutch female older singer tells me: "I already had good insight into the lives of people of different ages and ethnic backgrounds. Now maybe even more so, but the greatest change Music Generations has brought about is that I now know them personally." (Interview)

Above all, the older Dutch-Dutch participants lack not only an intergenerational but also an intercultural network. (Interviews)

Through their interaction around their shared love of music, the participants learn about the life experiences of the others. They get the opportunity to see that certain beliefs are similar and that others may differ, but that is okay. The collaborative relationships are horizontal, non-hierarchical; the generations and cultures meet as equals. This way, MusicGenerations provides fertile ground for affective ties, if not friendship, to blossom. (Observations, interviews)

The intense collaboration between the old and young talents in MusicGenerations—rehearsing their duets and collectively working toward powerful group performances during concerts—triggered a positive change in perceptions and attitudes, or at least, resulted in a stronger appreciation of "the other." (Questionnaire)

The practice of MusicGenerations additionally provides depth to our understanding of how contact and encounters need to be facilitated to have a positive effect and what the higher goals of these encounters may be. First, it can be argued that MusicGenerations' way of mediating social relationships through music creates opportunities for positive contact (see McLaren, 2003, p. 913; Nussbaum, 2012; and chapter 6). It generates settings of conviviality, i.e., living together, sharing, and interacting. And it does so between individuals whose social networks rarely overlap. "Talent for Freedom" shows that successful incentives for such interactions start from something people have in common: in this case, the love of music, a passion for singing, and the value the participants collectively attach to freedom.

Second, MusicGenerations illustrates that the goal need not be the evening out of difference. Political-ideological conceptions of social cohesion and assimilation often (implicitly) express the wish to "smooth out" society, to substitute difference with homogeneity. This wish prevails when difference is seen as a threat to society's internal social stability. MusicGenerations takes differences as a starting point, because it is a fact of everyday life in the cities they work in. MusicGenerations neither ignores nor reinforces difference, but looks instead for commonalities and shared ground on which to start a conversation. In doing so, it conceptualises difference—and the ensuing confrontations—as necessary elements to keep society and individual citizens sharp and self-reflexive.

Third, in many policies and (funding) programmes, the encounter itself seems to be the goal. But why stop there and just hope that mutual perceptions improve? MusicGenerations brings together a diversity of people with the aim to achieve a higher goal: collectively spreading the message of a caring and inclusive society. This is clearly just one option; it could also be an incentive to community organising or other forums in which people actively and collectively work on shared rights, shared interests, or to improve their (physical, political, cultural, or social) surroundings.

By Way of Conclusion: Towards Relational, Non-Emotional Bonds

Citizenship and national culture have become associated with the "emotional experience of citizens" (Frosh, 2001) in an "imagined community" defined by the boundaries of the nation state (Anderson, 1983). A shared identity, a homogeneous national culture, shared values: they have never truly been the basis of European national states. But this fact has never disrupted the strong belief in their existence. When we become fully aware of our society's total state of diversity, we will be able to realise that these notions cannot be the foundation of a future concept of citizenship. This chapter suggests a movement of both social cohesion and citizenship away from the realm of cultural and identity politics. It suggests taking the "emotional" out of citizenship. Because when citizenship is directly related to identity, it is indeed emotional: then citizenship is about who you are, what you stand for. Consequently, you won't like giving that up, or you will perceive of sharing your citizenship with "others" as impossible. You might even be willing "to die for your country"—even if the reason for your dying is grounded in an oversimplified story aimed at triggering an emotional reaction among the population. It is also the emotional aspect politicians hit on when they allude to the "immigrant threat" suggesting that it will "undermine our culture and who we are."

If we unmask citizenship, get rid of the cultural identity shroud under which the concept has lain smothered, we may finally be able to return to its essence: democracy, the principle of equality, and anti-discrimination. Rather than a form of identity-politics, citizenship could become a formal construct again, adhering to a democratic culture. This would imply that we refocus our communal attention on the basic elements of citizenship: civil, political and social rights, related responsibilities, and a just distribution of resources. The public sphere is then reserved for democratic culture and relationships built around shared interests or needs. Despite their backgrounds or identities, people can begin forming alliances around these. They collectively raise their voices to defend freedom, because otherwise none of us will be free. They collectively fight discrimination, irrespective of which personal characteristic they were discriminated against in the labour market or elsewhere: their faith, ethnicity, age, gender, sexual orientation, physical or mental challenge, and so on. Whatever triggered the discrimination; in all these instances the principle of equality is breached. And just as with freedom: that concerns us all.

Similarly, Harell and Stolle suggest redefining social cohesion in relational terms:

As a set of social relations that are characterized by people's ability to collaborate with one another to solve collective issues and to conduct dialogue in a way that does not privilege one social group's identity or perspective over another. (...) we propose a refined definition of social cohesion as cooperative relations among individuals and groups of individuals that are based on mutual recognition, equality and norms of reciprocity. We see such relations as defining a socially cohesive community and necessary for both the peaceful and democratic functioning of localities, states and even supranational communities. (2011, p. 17—original emphasis)

Such relational models of social cohesion are also being built in other studies of diversity as social practice, for instance by Padilla and colleagues (2014, pp. 1-8) and by Blommaert (2013). They borrow from Gilroy's concept of "conviviality" (2004):

a relational approach of interactions among individuals of different backgrounds, aiming at understanding how commonplace interactions between diverse populations occur
in a given context on a daily basis.

Vergès (2002) suggests how relationality could function at the national level. With the concept of "creole cosmopolitanism," she envisions a future in which it is accepted that humanity is diverse, that identities are multiple and based on relationships rather than on affiliation, blood, ancestry, or land. The latter may well remain important to one's individual identity, but relationships between people will rather be based on, e.g., shared public interest. As such, these relationships are non-emotional. In the context of such relationships, Harell and Stolle maintain that in a socially cohesive society "we find a lack of structural inequalities, a willingness of majorities and minorities alike to build non-hierarchical relationships, and related values of cooperation, mutual recognition, and support for democratic equality fairly evenly spread throughout" (2011, p. 22). With equality, democracy, and reciprocity, they hit on several prerequisites for citizenship, and thus, on basic citizenship skills all citizens should master. Several scholars have come up with comparable lists of values in their studies of contemporary citizenship (see for a partial overview Gowricharn, Postma, & Trienekens 2012). A useful contribution of Harell and Stolle is their interpretation of these values as "facilitative": "We view such values as secondary values, which people can endorse despite internal difference that may divide the population with respect to core values about religion, world view or preferences about the proper way to live one's life" (2011, p. 20).

Obviously, "culture" as such does not disappear. As Vergès pointed out, people's ethnic or cultural roots may constitute an important part of their individual identities, a part that receives appropriate recognition from follow citizens. As long as national states still play an important role in the organisation of citizenship, as long as national borders predominantly demarcate the area in which legislation and languages are effective, national cultures will not disappear. But citizens will perceive of this culture as being shaped and constantly reshaped by all citizens. This is a divergence from the notion of assimilation, because the new culture that is produced by the collective reshaping will differ from all cultures involved in the process. This is also a divergence from the notion of the "multicultural society." Although "multiculturalism" is still accepted and even further developed as a sociological concept in the Anglo-Saxon world (Boese & Phillips, 2015; Wise & Velayutham 2009), Dutch scholars signal a dire need for a "post-multicultural strategy" in the context of the Netherlands (Nicholls & Uitermark, 2013; Prins, 2013; Crul et al., 2013). Özdil (2015) shows that multiculturalism in the Dutch context—from populist right-wing to progressive political parties—has come to equal

In a relational, non-emotional practice of citizenship, there will be an inclusive understanding of who is considered "Dutch".

the insistence on segregation and co-existence rather than the mixing of people. In a relational, non-emotional practice of citizenship, citizens have a deep understanding that national cultures have always been the result of the mixing of cultures and habits of groups of people that were all, at one point in history, perceived as too distinct to ever be merged with the majority. In a relational, non-emotional practice of citizenship, there will be an inclusive understanding of who is considered "Dutch". Like the image presented by MusicGenerations' participants: "The Netherlands, the Dutch: that is all of us." Or as the former queen was heard saying after she attended a "Talent for Freedom" concert: "I was moved to tears. This is the way it should be: everybody together."

Over a decade ago, I drew attention to the "cultural" in citizenship. I introduced the notion of "lived citizenship," which I understood as a process that is "perpetually shaped and contested by everyday practices and informed by the dynamics in the cultural characteristics of citizenship such as identity and feelings of belonging" (Trienekens, 2004, p. 17). The extension "such as identity and feelings of belonging" indicates that I too applied an ethnic lens. With society's state of total diversity, I believe that lived citizenship could today be better envisioned as:

Lived citizenship refers to the equal rights and responsibilities of the people of a country who are held together primarily by relational, non-emotional bonds. The public sphere is reserved for democratic culture and relations are built around shared interests or needs by people irrespective of the shape of their intersecting, multi-layered identities. The country's culture—that which the current national culture eventually evolves into and which possibly continues to distinguish these people from people in other countries—is itself perpetually reshaped by everyday inclusive practices, in which everyone who is born and raised or who otherwise settles in the country mixes.

Then, the current "small realities" will have become the dominant one.

References

Allport, G. W. (1954). *The nature of prejudice.* Cambridge, MA: Perseus Books.

Anderson, B. (1983). *Imagined communities: Reflections on the origin and spread of nationalism.* London: Verso Editions.

Anthias, F. (1992). *Ethnicity, class, gender and migration: Greek Cypriots in Britain.* Aldershot: Avebury.

Anthias, F. (2012). Transnational mobilities, Migration research and intersectionality: Towards a translocational frame. *Nordic Journal of Migration Research*, 2(2), 102–120.

Anthias, F. & Yuval Davis, N. (1983). Contextualising feminism: Gender, ethnic and class divisions. *Feminist Review*, 15, 62–75.

Anthias, F. & Yuval Davis, N. (1992). *Racialised boundaries: Race, nation, gender, colour and class and the anti-racist struggle.* London: Routledge.

Arnaut, K. (2012). Super-diversity: Elements of an emerging perspective. *Diversities*, 14(2), 1–17.

Beck, U. (2006). *The Cosmopolitan Vision.* Cambridge: Polity.

Blommaert, J. (2013, April). Superdiversiteit en convivialiteit. *Republiek Allochtonië*, 21.

Boese, M. & Phillips, M. (2015). Looking beyond multicultural performance: Multiculturalising as deliberate process of engagement and negotiation. In: F. Mansouri (Ed.), *Cultural, religious and political contestations: The multicultural challenge* (pp. 205–222). Switzerland: Springer International.

Brah, A. (1992). Difference, diversity and differentiation. In J. Donald & A. Rattansi (Eds.), *"Race," culture, difference.* London: Sage.

Buck-Morss, S. (2014). Democracy: An unfinished project. *boundary 2*, 41(2), 71–98.

CERD (2015, June). *Rapportage: Aan de 87e zitting van het VN-Comité inzake de uitbanning van alle vormen van Rassendiscriminatie (CERD) ten behoeve van de behandeling van de 19e–21e rapporten van Nederland.* Utrecht: College voor de Rechten van de Mens.

Collins, H. (1993). Toward a new vision: Race, class and gender as categories of analysis and connection. *Race, Sex and Class*, 1(1), 25–45.

Crenshaw, K. (1994). Mapping the margins: Intersectionality, identity politics and violence against women of color. In: M. Fineman & R. Mykitiuk (Eds.), *The public nature of private violence* (pp. 93–118). New York: Routlegde.

Crul, M., Schneider, J., & Lelie, F. (2013). *Super diversiteit.* Amsterdam: VU University Press.

Doucerain, M., Dere, J., & Ryder, A. (2013). Travels in hyper-diversity: Multiculturalism and the contextual assessment of acculturation. *International Journal of Intercultural Relations*, 37, 686–699.

dvhn.nl (2015, December 21). Gebroederlijk kerstfeest op terrein azc Oranje. *Dagblad van het Noorden*. Consulted on 23 February 2016.

Essed, P. (1991). *Understanding everyday racism: An interdisciplinary theory.* London: Sage.

Essed, P. (2001). Multi-identifications and transformations: Reaching beyond racial and ethnic reductionisms. *Social Identities*, 7(4), 493–509.

Flint, J., & Robinson, D. (Eds.) (2008). *Community cohesion in crisis? New dimensions of diversity and difference*. Bristol: Policy Press.

Frosh, S. (2001). Psychoanalysis, identity and citizenship. In N. Stevenson (Ed.), *Culture and citizenship* (pp. 62–73). London: Sage.

Ghorashi, H. (2010). *Culturele diversiteit: Nederlandse identiteit en democratisch burgerschap. Multiculturele samenleving in ontwikkeling, deel 4*. Den Haag: Sdu Uitgevers.

Gidley, B. (2013). Landscapes of belonging, portraits of life: Researching everyday multiculture in an inner city estate. *Identities: Global Studies in Culture and Power*, 20(4), 361–376.

Gilroy, P. (2004). *After empire: Melancholia or convivial culture?* London: Routledge.

Gowricharn, R. (2015). Sociability networks of migrant youngsters: The case of Dutch Hindustanis. *Current Sociology*. 1–18. doi:10.1177/0011392115605628

Gowricharn, R., Postma, D. W., & Trienekens, S. (Eds). (2011). *Geleefd Burgerschap: Van eenheidsdwang naar ruimte voor verschil en vitaliteit*. Amsterdam: SWP.

Granovetter, M. (1973). The strength of weak ties. *American Journal of Sociology*, 78(6), 1360–1380.

Hagestad, G., & Uhlenberg, P. (2006). Should we be concerned about age segregation? Some theoretical and empirical explorations. *Research on Aging*, 28(6), 638–653.

Hardt, M., & Negri, A. (2000). *Empire*. Cambridge, MA: Harvard University Press.

Harell, A., & Stolle, D. (2011). Reconciling diversity and community? Defining social cohesion in democracies. In M. Hooghe (Ed.), *Theoretical perspectives on social cohesion and social capital* (pp. 8–43). Brussels: Royal Flemish Academy of Belgium for Science and the Arts.

Heijne, B. (2012). *Development cooperation, humanism, crisis: Where to from here?* Den Haag: Hivos, The Knowledge Programme.

Heijne, B. (2016, January 2). Niet langer verbonden. *NRC Weekend*, 20–21.

Hewstone, M., Tausch, N., et al. (2007). Identity, ethnic diversity and community cohesion. In M. Wetherell, M. Lafleche, & R. Berkeley (Eds.), *Identity, ethnic diversity and community cohesion* (pp. 102–112). Los Angeles, CA: Sage.

Lucassen, J., & Penninx, R. (1997). *Newcomers. immigrants and their descendants in the Netherlands 1550-1995*. Amsterdam: Het Spinhuis.

Lucassen, L. (2005). *The Immigrant Threat*. Champaign: IL: University of Illinois Press.

McLaren, L. M. (2003). Anti-immigrant prejudice in Europe: Contact, threat perception, and preferences for the exclusion of migrants. *Social Forces*, 81, 909–936.

Meissner, F. (2014). Migration in migration-related diversity? The nexus between superdiversity and migration studies. *Ethnic and Racial Studies*. doi:10.1080/01419870.2015.970209

Nicholls, W., & Uitermark, J. (2013). Post-multicultural cities: A comparison of minority politics in Amsterdam and L.A. *Journal of Ethnic and Racial Studies*, 39.

Noble, G. (2011). Belonging in Bennelong: Ironic inclusion and cosmopolitan joy in John Howard's (former) electorate. In K. Jacobs & J. Malpas (Eds.), Ocean to outback: *Cosmopolitanism in contemporary Australia* (pp. 150–174). Perth: UWA Press.

Nussbaum, M. (2012). *The new religious intolerance: Overcoming the politics of fear in an anxious society.* Cambridge, MA: Harvard University Press.

Özdil, Z. (2015). *Nederland mijn vaderland.* Amsterdam: De Bezige Bij.

Padilla, B., Azevedo, J., & Olmos-Alcaraz, A. (2014). Superdiversity and conviviality: Exploring frameworks for doing ethnography in Southern European intercultural cities. *Ethnic and Racial Studies.* doi:10.1080/01419870.2015.980294

Parkin, D., & Arnaut, K. (2012). *Super-diversity, a digest.* Göttingen: Max Planck Institute for the Study of Religious and Ethnic Diversity.

Prins, B. (2013, June 10). Niet multicultureel maar superdivers! *Republiek Allochtonië.*

RtvDrenthe.nl. (2016). Boze inwoners Oranje belagen staatssecretaris: Vrouw raakt gewond. *RtvDrenthe.nl*, 6 October 2015. Consulted on 23 February 2016.

Savelkoul, M., Scheepers, P., Tolsma, J., & Hagendoorn, L. (2011). Anti-Muslim attitudes in The Netherlands: Tests of contradictory hypotheses derived from ethnic competition theory and intergroup contact theory. *European Sociological Review*, 27(6), 741–758.

SCP. (2008). *Betrekkelijke Betrokkenheid: Studies in sociale cohesie.*
Sociaal en Cultureel Rapport 2008. Den Haag: Sociaal Cultureel Planbureau.

Solomos, J. (2001). Race, multi-culturalism and difference. In N. Stevenson (Ed.), *Culture and citizenship* (pp. 198–211). London: Sage.

Trienekens, S. (2004). *Urban paradoxes: Lived citizenship and the location of diversity in the arts.* Amsterdam: Trienekens.

Trienekens, S., & Hillaert, W. (2015). *Art in transition: Manifesto for participatory art practices.* Brussel: Demos/CAL-XL.

Vergès, F. (2002). Vertigo and emancipation: Creole cosmopolitanism and cultural politics. In S. Lash & M. Featherstone (Eds.), *Recognition and difference: Politics, identity, multiculture* (pp. 169–184). London: Sage.

Vertovec, S. (2007). Super-diversity and its implications. *Ethnic and Racial Studies*, 30(6), 1024–1054.

Vertovec, S. (2012). "Diversity" and the social imaginary. European *Journal of Sociology*, 53(3), 287–312.

Wekker, G. (1992). I am a gold coin: *The construction of selves, gender and sexualities in a female, working-class, Afro-Surinamese setting* (Doctoral dissertation). University of California, Los Angeles.

Wessendorf, S. (2013). Commonplace diversity and the "ethos of mixing": Perceptions of difference in a London neighbourhood. *Identities: Global Studies in Culture and Power*, 20(4), 407–422.

Wise, A., & Velayutham, S. (Eds.). (2009). *Everyday multiculturalism.* Basingstoke: Palgrave Macmillan.

Audience
Rotterdamse
Schouwburg

Yes-R
Talent for Freedom

PART III

IMPLICATIONS

11. Challenges for Policy, Funding, and Education

Sandra Trienekens

An inclusive understanding of our society's diversity

This multidisciplinary volume has illustrated the way in which MusicGenerations applies an inclusive view of diversity in society; how it embraces and promotes a vision of a diverse, caring society. Whereas it may not be unique in addressing the themes of age, generations, diversity, or freedom, it is in its multidimensional focus on all of these themes simultaneously. Consequently, it does not merely convey the message that old people are fun, talented, and can be extremely vital. MusicGenerations simultaneously speaks of super-diversity, places age in an intergenerational context, and addresses, together with its highly diverse group of vocal talents, pressing social issues.

Its practice makes us aware of "society's state of total diversity," in which even people from the former white majority no longer apply a one-dimensional frame of (national) cultural reference. It shows that the problem of segregation may be smaller than commonly perceived, and more importantly, that the "gap" seems to be easily closed when people are approached in the right manner. It shows that old and young people, as well as those of different cultural or socio-economic backgrounds, enjoy their collaboration. In the process, in the playful ritual collective singing represents, perceptions of the "other" change in a positive way.

MusicGenerations' concerts allow us to perceive people as individuals, rather than as group members. One quickly becomes aware that there is more to people's identity than just their age or ethnicity. It makes us aware of the complex, intersecting nature of our identities. It illustrates that, contrary to popular beliefs, homogeneity is not a prerequisite for unity. In a sufficiently mixed group, "difference" becomes quotidian and values other than those related to age, ethnic cultures, or religions begin to function as binding forces. What is more, the practice of MusicGenerations shows that mixing is already reality. Hence, MusicGenerations illustrates that the goal need not be the evening out of difference to maintain a stable society.

An effective approach

Not only is MusicGenerations inspiring with regard to its conceptualisation of society's diversity and the intersections among age, diversity, socio-economic backgrounds, musical taste, and the like. It also applies an inspiring approach. In MusicGenerations, people are approached as talents. The MusicGenerations team values the participants for who they are and what they (dis)like. The participants' talents are taken as a starting point, not their "problems," shortcomings, diversity, or age. As such, the arts are at the core of the programme, not care or welfare. It is about doing something the participants really like, about having fun. Moreover, MusicGenerations takes an intergenerational approach to age and works from the intersection of age, ethnicity, musical tastes, etc. It provides room for self-definition; the participants decide which part of their identity they will show on stage. Additionally, the generations, ethnicities, and cultures meet as equals; there is no hierarchy in talent, knowledge, or influence. To achieve collaboration and unity among such a diverse group of talents, the team positively exploits the power of music and the connecting power of the participants' shared love of music. This love allows the participants to recognise themselves in the others as well as to differ from them in taste, preference, or interpretation. This way, disagreement or difference does not stand in the way of successful collaboration. Consequently, the overall concept of the programme conveys a strong political message and a critical reflection on contemporary social practices.

Challenges

What practical challenges can be discerned for the MusicGenerations' organisation itself, for policy and funding, and for the education of the next generation of cultural and social workers?

For MusicGenerations

MusicGenerations is about to enter a new phase. Responding to the latest pressing societal issue, and given the end of the "Talent for Freedom" programme, the focus is shifting to inclusion of the refugees who have recently arrived in the Netherlands. The approach, as it developed over the past 15 years, will not need to change drastically. Like the migrant seniors of the past, the refugees of today will enjoy being approached as humans, as talents, as people who have brought with them a rich cultural heritage from their countries of origin. Recent steps toward a full-fledged programme and the first musical encounters between MusicGenerations and several groups of refugees indicate that this is indeed the case. The main challenge for the MusicGenerations organisation will be to sufficiently seek out the very heart of the proverbial crossfire among society's divided groups. Encounters and dialogue between refugees and Dutch people who welcome refugees to the Netherlands, however important, are not the ultimate aim. That aim is to incorporate into the programme those citizens who are passionately opposed to the accommodation of refugees, whose strong populist convictions and ways of reasoning do not necessarily comply with the rules of logic. It may prove a challenge to manage the strong emotions that may be unleashed.

In the meantime, another on-going challenge is to share the experiences gained and the approach built over 15 years of MusicGenerations with other social and cultural organisations across the country, and even abroad. In previous years, there have been a handful of national and international organisations that have been inspired, through their collaboration with MusicGenerations, to adopt an intergenerational approach in their programmes. But ideally, the number of organisations receptive to MusicGenerations' approach would further increase. One obstacle is the categorisation prevalent in the social and cultural sector, fed also by "target-group thinking" that continues to underlie most policies and funding schemes.

For Policies and Funding

The challenge for policy and funding bodies is to accept society's state of total diversity. It would signify a great step forward if we could refrain from categorizing people and thinking in terms of target groups in our policies; if we could come to accept that complexity is of such intricate nature that it is pointless to continue to label people along the lines of distinct categories, or to single out one specific category by which to describe an individual, such as age, ethnicity, or religion.

This volume shows that crosscutting "target groups" had positive effects and resulted in a noteworthy programme in the case of MusicGenerations. Positive outcomes have also been established in research: e.g., the elderly's negative attitudes toward youngsters were reversed, depression levels were decreased, and their self-esteem increased by participating in an intergenerational program; children's attitudes toward the elderly improved when taking part in such a program (Newman & Brummel, 1989). Such changes in attitudes can also have a positive impact on society, given that contact likely results in a more positive image of "others" and in willingness to help them. Crosscutting target groups thus helps to build the diverse networks our European societies so urgently require. At the very least, it prevents us from reinforcing the already existing segregation between groups.

Nonetheless, policies and funding programmes still tend to categorise people on the basis of one-dimensional conceptions of their identities: young people; seniors; "ethnic-minorities"; people living in diverse, local boroughs; and so on. For example, Rotterdam's cultural education policies are directed at the young people in the city. National talent development programmes are directed either at young people or professional artists; national programmes single out seniors and are predominantly framed in terms of care or welfare rather than talent development. However, awareness of the current complexity appears to be growing. For instance, the Ministry of Health and Welfare acknowledges that to maintain current standards, the different generations will have to care for each other given the present demography. Now, the time has come to design (cultural) policy and funding programmes that stimulate both the awareness and implementation of an enabling "total-diversity" and "shared passion not problem" approach.

For Cultural Organisations
Art projects can provide a way to build a communal basis, connection, and trust—needed to prevent further polarisation and to allow difference to become a positive quality of society. Although culture can also be a dividing force, MusicGenerations shows the way in which art (music) can have a binding quality. Our current minister of culture agrees when she writes that, with the reflection and imagination the arts bring to the table, old patterns can be broken and new relationships can be formed.

Programmes
We challenge cultural institutions to develop practices that are inclusive in terms of age, diversity, cultural taste, and talents. Programmes that do not take all these aspects into account can still be beneficial, but can be further strengthened by adopting the notion of total diversity and engaging a myriad of people. Ideally, these efforts would culminate in an annual event of the highest artistic quality in which intergenerationality and "total-diversity" is fully integrated in order to raise the profile and visibility of such an approach.

Getting there together
Cultural producers should be enabled to make inclusive programmes in collaboration with established cultural institutions and funding bodies. Up until now, these institutions have often been tied to long-term planning and funding objectives that leave little room for an intergenerational approach. Moreover, programmes should be rewarded when they stimulate their talents to participate in other talent development programmes too. This would allow them to develop their talent continuously.

Current practice is that cultural producers have to account for the number of people who remain in their programmes, preferably for a long time. It would be better if the cultural sector were to build a cluster of talent development programmes, each providing distinct opportunities for people of all ages and backgrounds.

For Education in Cultural and Social Work

For an inclusive society, we will obviously have to start at the basis of it all: education. Would it not be a great step forward if, in the near future, all pupils leaving school have learned about the history of slavery? Here we focus on higher education, and specifically, on the next generation of social and cultural professionals. They too should be positioned to obtain a deeper understanding of society's total state of diversity and of the benefits of transcending target group thinking. During their studies, they should be stimulated to familiarise themselves with art programmes such as those described in this volume and with the "total-diversity" and "shared passion not problem" approach as developed by, for instance, MusicGenerations: to address people as talented individuals and seduce them, by tapping into their passions, into interacting with others in non-hierarchical ways. The objective is to facilitate factual encounters; not to stop there, but to collectively present an alternative to society's ills. A second objective is to engage people in activities they freely and positively choose to be part of and in which they can use their skills. And thus, to refrain from designing activities or programmes in which people are approached as members of "groups in need" and which primarily result from the (dominant) moral convictions of the social and cultural professionals themselves.

References Newman, S., & Brummel, S. (1989). *Intergenerational programs: Imperatives, strategies, impacts, trends.* London: The Haworth Press.

Serdi
Talent for Freedom

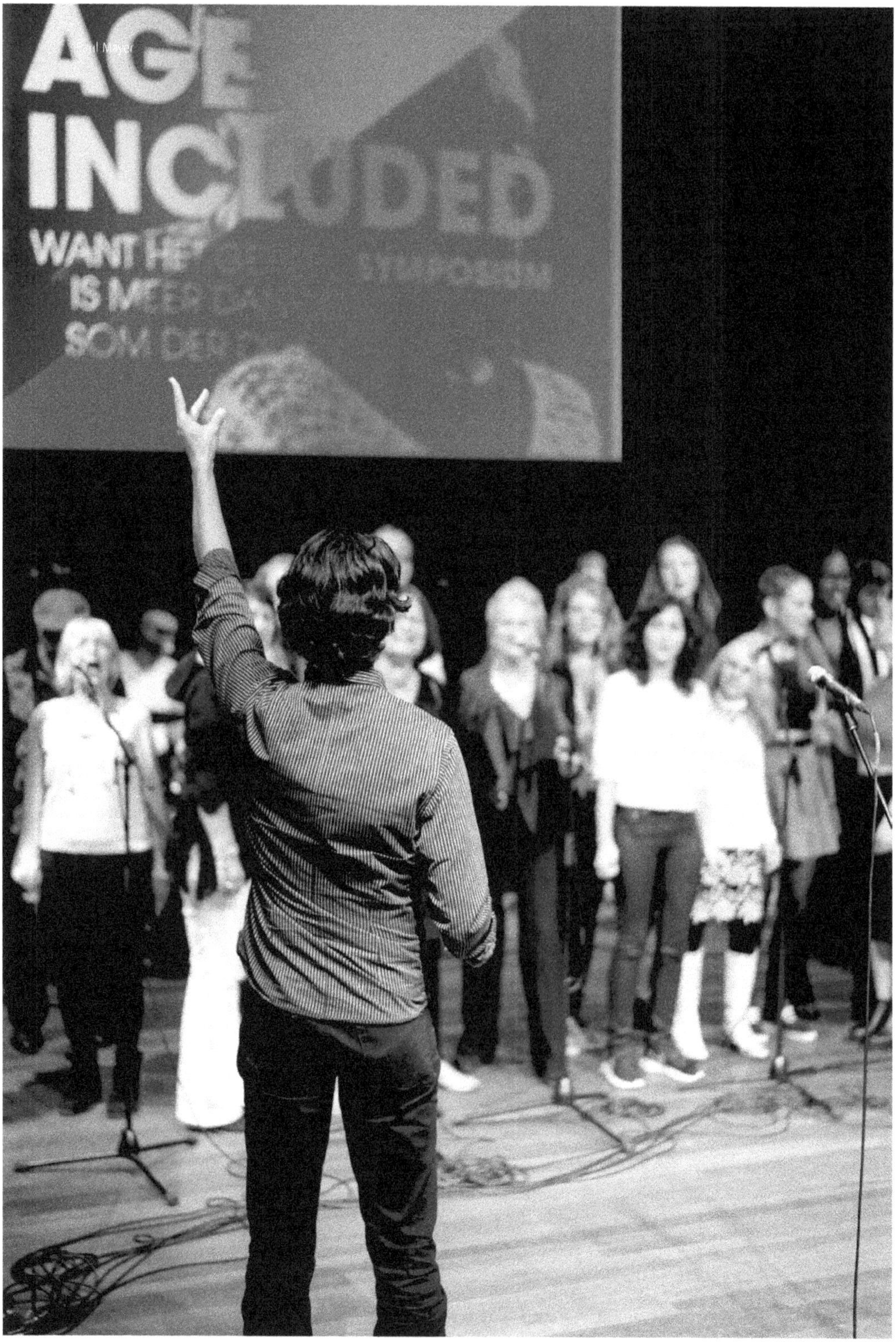
AGE
INCLUDED
SYMPOSIUM

APPENDIXES

I Music Generations: People & Figures

People

Conny Groot is the founder of the Euro+ Songfestival Foundation. She is the director and beating heart of the MusicGenerations programme. Paul Mayer has been MusicGenerations' music director since 2007. A lean and mean team, consisting of one office manager and two annual interns, backs up Groot and Mayer. They are assisted periodically by designers of flyers and the website, a director to set the productions and festivals, a producer to help organise major events, and a PR specialist who coordinates social media and press releases.

A band of music students supports the vocal talents during rehearsals and concerts. They are recruited at the music academies of the cities in which MusicGenerations' programmes take place, such as the Rotterdam music academy Codart s, Hanze Hogeschool Groningen and several pop academies. Local social and cultural organisations assist in communication with and recruiting of participants, and promote the concerts to their communities. MusicGenerations contacts approximately 140 intermediaries and organisations a year. Over the years, reciprocal relationships have developed with several of them.

Figures 2001–2015

Estimated total participants: 2000
Participants' age: 65 per cent are over 55; 35 per cent are under 25 years of age Dutch participants of colour: 70 per cent
Estimated audience: 65,000
(Inter)national locations where programmes took place: 35
Estimated funding over 15 years: 1.5 million

Funding bodies that have (regularly) supported MusicGenerations over the past 15 years: Fonds voor Cultuurparticipatie, Fonds Sluyterman van Loo, RCOAK, VSBfonds, Prins Bernhard Cultuurfonds, Gemeente Amsterdam Stadsdeel Nieuw West, Rotterdam Festivals / Gemeente Rotterdam. Partner venues such as the theatres De Meervaart, Rotterdamse Schouwburg and Theater Zuidplein support MusicGenerations in kind. The Euro+ Songfestival Foundation has the "ANBI" status.

II About the authors

The authors' backgrounds & their roles in the conference "Age Included"

Eltje Bos is professor of Cultural and Social Dynamics at the Amsterdam University of Applied Sciences. She was keynote speaker at the Age Included conference.

Maurice Crul is professor of Sociology and holds the chair for Diversity and Education at the Free University of Amsterdam and the Erasmus University Rotterdam. He was keynote speaker at the Age Included conference.

Conny Groot holds an M.A. in Theatre Studies, and in European Art and Media Management. She is director of MusicGenerations and founder of the Euro+ Songfestival Foundation. Like everyone else at MusicGenerations, she is self-employed and also regularly develops community programs for other foundations. She organised the Age Included conference and is co-editor of this volume.

Marjolein Gysels, Ph.D., is an anthropologist and works at the University of Amsterdam. Her research is on participatory art with older people and people with demetia. During the Age Included conference, she conducted a workshop on this topic together with Laurien Mulder, a visual artist from Zona's Kiosk.

Zihni Özdil, M.A., is a historian, columnist, and author. His latest book is Nederland mijn Vaderland (The Netherlands, my Fatherland). He is lecturer of Global History at the Erasmus University Rotterdam and a columnist for the Dutch newspaper NRC Handelsblad. He moderated the Age Included conference.

Ger Tielen is director of Demin, a consultancy agency supporting initiatives dealing with demographic developments from the perspective of age-diversity and solidarity between the generations. He is chairman of the board of the Euro+ Songfestival Foundation.

Sandra Trienekens, Ph.D., is a political geographer and cultural sociologist, and director of Urban Paradoxes, a research agency at the crossroads of art and society. She conducted research on the "Talent for Freedom" programme, commissioned by MusicGenerations. She was keynote speaker at the Age Included conference and is co-editor of this volume.

Co-authors/research assistants

Britt Swartjes studies Sociology at Radboud University Nijmegen and is an intern at Urban Paradoxes (February–July 2016).

Milda Saltenyte was a student of the Research Master Social Sciences in 2014-2015 at the University of Amsterdam, during which time she did a two-month internship at Urban Paradoxes.

Talent for Freedom
with refugees

This publication was made possible by:

VSBfonds

Fonds voor Cultuurparticipatie

Rotterdam Festivals

RCOAK

Fonds Sluyterman van Loo

Prins Bernhard Cultuurfonds

Theater de Meervaart

We would like to extend our gratitude to: Ingeborg Wegter, Freddy May, Ger Tielen, Romy Jochems and Ruben Gowricharn.

Title	**AGE INCLUDED ON MUSIC, GENERATIONS, DIVERSITY AND FREEDOM**
Editors	*Sandra Trienekens & Conny Groot*
ISBN	978 90 8850 689 5
e-ISBN	978 90 8850 690 1
NUR	757
Cover picture	Hilde Speet
Pictures	Antoinette van Oort, Sterk-Werk, Bosse Beckers, Hilde Speet
Design	Studio Kattekwaad - www.studiokattekwaad.nl

For information on other SWP Publications:

P.O.Box 12010, 1100 AA Amsterdam-Zuidoost

Tel.: + 31 (0)20 330 72 00

Email: contact@mailswp.com

Internet: www.swpbook.com

www.ingramcontent.com/pod-product-compliance
Lightning Source LLC
Chambersburg PA
CBHW081827170426
43202CB00019B/2974